Design and Build Your Ideal Entertainment Center

BY POPULAR WOODWORKING BOOKS

POPULAR WOODWORKING BOOKS
CINCINNATI, OHIO
www.popularwoodworking.com

Design and Build Your Ideal Entertainment Center Copyright © 2004
by Popular Woodworking Books. Manufactured in China. All rights reserved.
No part of this book may be reproduced in any form or by any electronic or
mechanical means, including information storage and retrieval systems, without permission in writing from the publisher, except by a reviewer, who may
quote brief passages in a review. Published by Popular Woodworking Books,
an imprint of F&W Publications, Inc., 4700 East Galbraith Road, Cincinnati,
Ohio, 45236. (800) 289-0963. First edition.

Visit our Web site at www.popularwoodworking.com for information on more
resources for woodworkers.

Other fine Popular Woodworking Books are available from your local bookstore or direct from the publisher.

09   08   07   06   05   6   5   4   3   2

Library of Congress Cataloging-in-Publication Data

Design and build your ideal entertainment center / by Popular Woodworking
Books.p. cm.
   Includes index.
   ISBN 13: 978-1-55870-697-2 (alk. paper)
   ISBN 10: 1-55870-697-6 (alk. paper)
   1. Entertainment centers (Cabinetwork) I. Popular Woodworking Books
(Firm)
TT197.5.E5H69 2004
684.1'6--dc22   2003062337

ACQUISITIONS EDITOR: Jim Stack
EDITED BY: Jennifer Ziegler
DESIGNED BY: Brian Roeth
PRODUCTION COORDINATED BY: Robin Richie
LAYOUT ARTIST: Christine Long

METRIC CONVERSION CHART

TO CONVERT	TO	MULTIPLY BY
Inches	Centimeters	2.54
Centimeters	Inches	0.4
Feet	Centimeters	30.5
Centimeters	Feet	0.03
Yards	Meters	0.9
Meters	Yards	1.1
Sq. Inches	Sq. Centimeters	6.45
Sq. Centimeters	Sq. Inches	0.16
Sq. Feet	Sq. Meters	0.09
Sq. Meters	Sq. Feet	10.8
Sq. Yards	Sq. Meters	0.8
Sq. Meters	Sq. Yards	1.2
Pounds	Kilograms	0.45
Kilograms	Pounds	2.2
Ounces	Grams	28.4
Grams	Ounces	0.035

acknowledgements

>> The editors of Popular Woodworking books would like to thank the following woodworkers whose work is featured in this book — Glen Huey, Danny Proulx, Jim Stack, Jim Stuard, Troy Sexton, Rick Williams and Amy Zimmer.

READ THIS IMPORTANT SAFETY NOTICE

To prevent accidents, keep safety in mind while you work. Use the safety guards installed on power equipment; they are for your protection. When working on power equipment, keep fingers away from saw blades, wear safety goggles to prevent injuries from flying wood chips and sawdust, wear headphones to protect your hearing, and consider installing a dust vacuum to reduce the amount of airborne sawdust in your woodshop. Don't wear loose clothing, such as neckties or shirts with loose sleeves, or jewelry, such as rings, necklaces or bracelets, when working on power equipment. Tie back long hair to prevent it from getting caught in your equipment. People who are sensitive to certain chemicals should check the chemical content of any product before using it. The authors and editors who compiled this book have tried to make the contents as accurate and correct as possible. Plans, illustrations, photographs and text have been carefully checked. All instructions, plans and projects should be carefully read, studied and understood before beginning construction. Due to the variability of local conditions, construction materials, skill levels, etc., neither the author nor Popular Woodworking Books assumes any responsibility for any accidents, injuries, damages or other losses incurred resulting from the material presented in this book. Prices listed for supplies and equipment were current at the time of publication and are subject to change. Glass shelving should have all edges polished and must be tempered. Untempered glass shelves may shatter and can cause serious bodily injury. Tempered shelves are very strong and if they break will just crumble, minimizing personal injury.

CONTENTS

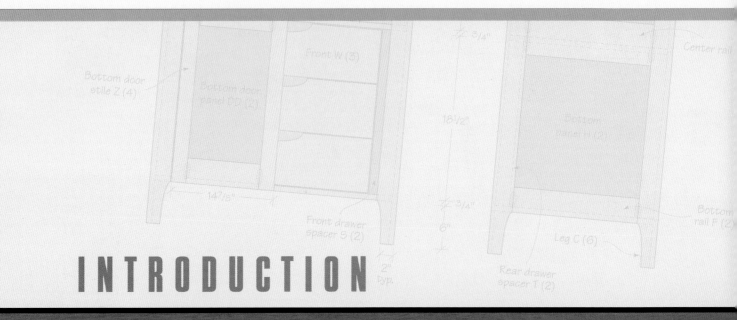

INTRODUCTION

>> During the 1940s and early 1950s, television was invented and went into development. Little did the pioneers involved in this new form of electronic communication know how their hard work would change the lives of people for generations yet to come.

Anyone born after 1956 will not remember when there weren't color televisions. For better or worse, television programming became the focus of wireless communication, complete with new ways of presenting news and current events, dramas, game shows, situation comedies, etc. Companies with products to sell found a way to advertise and sell their products as never before. Life as most people knew it was changed forever.

We have entered the 21st century and with us have come more electronic gadgets than anyone could have predicted. We still watch television and listen to music, but now we can bring almost any movie into our homes to view anytime we choose. In addition, computers have risen so much in popularity as to vie with television for our attention.

Computers will soon be the heart of our visual and audio communication. The entertainment centers we build today will house a central unit that will play DVDs, CDs, videocassettes, audiotapes and also control World Wide Web, cable and/or satellite feeds into our homes via television. It's entirely possible the number of components used in entertainment centers will decrease to one component and a large video

screen. This system will have speakers to carry the sound around the room.

The first chapter of this book discusses the hows and whys of entertainment center design. An entertainment center can become a whole wall of bookcases and storage cabinets that adds a totally new function to a room.

The projects are arranged from a simple corner unit to a more complex unit that has separate cabinets for various components. All the project designs are meant to spark your creative thoughts so you can adapt them to your own personal needs. Feel free to change dimensions, styles, materials used or anything else that strikes your fancy.

All the projects in this book have been "field tested," so we know they work. The methods of construction vary, giving you a choice of mortise-and-tenon, biscuit, dowel and other types of joinery. When it comes to finishing your project, you'll see stain, lacquer, polyurethane and paint. All materials are readily available at home-improvement centers, local hardware stores and on-line. A list of suppliers is furnished at the end of the book to help you find and choose just the right materials you'll need to build your projects.

We hope that you have fun designing, building and using your new entertainment center.

designing
the perfect

WHERE TO START

During the design and planning stages of making an entertainment center for your home, you need to answer several questions. Where will the unit be located? How will it be used? What equipment will it house? Will it be a freestanding or built-in cabinet?

Many of us already have a television and possibly a stereo. VCR and CD players are common, as well as some type of cable or satellite dish for our televisions. Add to that a computer, video game components, DVD player, surround sound system, large-screen television and it becomes important to have a place to house all this equipment!

Location Is Everything

The location of the entertainment center is the first consideration. If the room is small, a small cabinet is a natural choice. But even in a small cabinet, a surprising amount of storage space is possible. If the television is placed on top of the cabinet, there is ample room for a cable box, DVD and VCR players and a storage drawer.

A larger room has more space, which opens up more possibilities for an entertainment center. One idea would be to dedicate a corner or one end of the room to TV viewing and video games. A medium-size cabinet that doubles as a piece of furniture would be a good choice in this situation. When the unit is not in use, it will look great just being in the room. Another idea is to make the entertainment center the focus of the room. A larger cabinet could be made to house a larger television and possibly some surround sound system components.

In a very large room, the possibilities are almost unlimited. A medium-size cabinet is always a good choice. Or a whole wall fitted out with bookcases, a desk and/or storage cabinets and a cabinet for a large-screen television is possible. If you really like the feel of a movie theater and want to re-create that feel, large front- or rear-projection screens are available, complete with all the speakers, amplifiers and video components needed. Add to that a popcorn cart, pop machine, used theater seats and several friends and you're in business!

Will It All Fit?

After you've picked your location, it's time to count all your components. Do you want them all in the same place? Probably, but you might want the video games used in another location, for example. Are you planning on adding to your component collections or replacing them? The important part is to be sure that all the components will fit

entertainment center for your home

A freestanding entertainment center is a piece of furniture. As such, it can decorate a room when not in use.

into the entertainment center you're going to build.

Measure each component's height, width and depth (don't forget the television). The space needed for the components will vary, so use the largest component's measurements as your standard for sizing the interior of the cabinet. Most manuals that come with components will indicate how much space is needed for air circulation. Add these numbers to the inside dimensions of the cabinet. If you know, or even think, you will be purchasing new components in the future, allow a little extra room inside the cabinet just in case the new component is larger than the one it will replace.

One other consideration when planning your entertainment center is the layout and routes of the wiring for all the components. Shelves that hold the components commonly have one back corner clipped off; a $1\frac{1}{2}$"–2"-diameter hole is drilled toward the back of the shelf; or the shelf is cut $1\frac{1}{2}$" narrower than needed and two wings are added to the back edge of the shelf, bringing it to full depth and leaving a $1\frac{1}{2}$"-wide

entertainment center facts

>> • Cabinets that house televisions need to be at least
24" to 26" deep. Take this into account when planning where the cabinet will sit or be installed. Measure the television that will be going into the
cabinet to be absolutely sure of the cabinet depth.
Remember to include the thickness of the doors and
the back of the cabinet.

• Always measure every piece of electronic equipment
that will be going into a media center before you
cut any materials!

• Inserts that fit into drawers and hold DVDs, CDs,
videocassettes and audiocassettes are the best way
to store these items. These inserts can be purchased
from most woodworking and cabinetmaking suppliers (see suppliers list in the back of the book). For
those of you who want to build your own drawer
dividers, here are the specifications:

	T	(mm)	W	(mm)	H	(mm)
CDs	$7/16$"	(11)	$4^{15}/_{16}$"	(125)	$5^5/_8$"	(143)
DVDs	$5/8$"	(16)	$5^3/_8$"	(137)	$7^1/_2$"	(191)
VIDEOTAPES	1"	(25)	$7^9/_{16}$"	(192)	$4^1/_8$"	(105)
RECORD ALBUMS	$3/16$"	(5)	$12^3/_8$"	(314)	$12^3/_8$"	(314)
AUDIOCASSETTES	$11/16$"	(18)	$4^5/_{16}$"	(110)	$2^3/_4$"	(70)

Built-in entertain-
ment centers
become part of
a room and ulti-
mately the build-
ing itself. They
blend seamlessly
into the walls and
sometimes the
ceiling, also.

slot at the back of the shelf. These techniques can be used to create access through vertical cabinet dividers to connect one section of a cabinet to another or to create access between adjoining cabinets.

If you haven't started sketching yet, now is the time to start. Draw a box to represent the cabinet for the components. Draw another box for the TV. Draw other boxes if you want space for storage, speakers, books or whatever. If you draw them to scale, it will help you visualize the proportions of each box as it relates to the others.

Choosing a Furniture Style

As you're gathering all your information, you'll need to decide on a furniture style that you want to use for the entertainment center. Where the center is located is usually the key factor in making this decision. If other pieces of furniture are in the room, do you want them to match the entertainment center? If you've decided you want built-in cabinets, they should match the style of the room. You can use the same type of mouldings and colors of paint or stain. This will help the cabinets blend into the room nicely.

Another factor in choosing a style is knowing your woodworking skill levels.

cabinet depth

>> As a general rule, cabinets that are deeper than 24" will make a room feel smaller. They actually take 2' from the space of the room. This is sometimes hard to visualize, and only when the cabinets have been built and installed do people realize they've boxed themselves into a room. If a room is to become a den or library and you want bookcases all around the room, they should not be any deeper than 12". Bookcases that are 10" deep will hold all but the largest books, though you will have to build shelves 24"-26" deep for a television set.

Making a knockdown entertainment center is a good way to make a larger unit that can be transported easily.

A smaller entertainment center can be your answer in a small room.

You should build something you're comfortable making (that's not to say you can't try a new technique or two). Building a piece of furniture is a challenge on any level and you don't want to become discouraged halfway through the project. This book presents several different styles to help you decide if one of them will fit your needs.

This critical step will help you determine how much material and what kinds and amounts of hardware will be needed, as well as the cost of all these things.

Pulling It All Together

Now that you have the entertainment center's location, the number and type of components that will be housed in it, the style, types of materials and a good working drawing(s), you're all set to create a cutting list of materials.

This critical step will help you determine how much material will be needed, what kinds and amounts of hardware and the cost of all these things. It's this step that often gets only a cursory run-through.

When creating a cutting list, you are prebuilding the whole project in your mind and on paper. It's at this point that you will discover what sizes to cut your parts, what joinery will

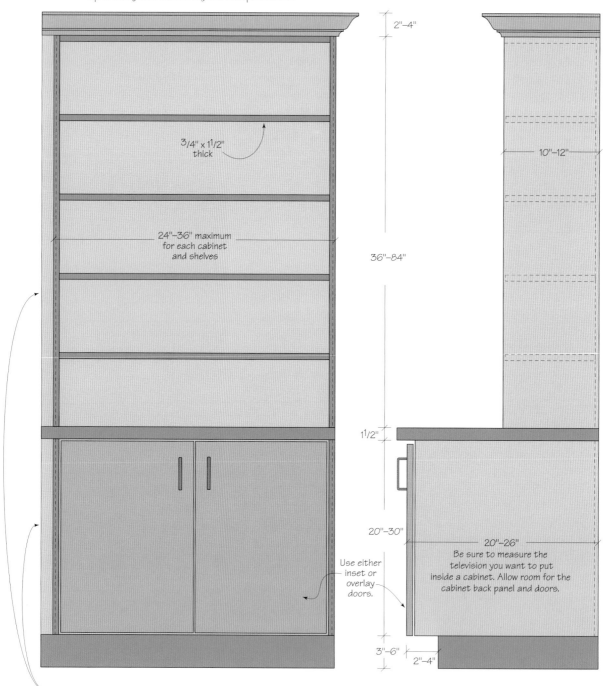

Top moulding runs the full length of multiple cabinets.

3/4" x 1 1/2" thick

24"–36" maximum for each cabinet and shelves

2"–4"

10"–12"

36"–84"

1 1/2"

20"–30"

20"–26"
Be sure to measure the television you want to put inside a cabinet. Allow room for the cabinet back panel and doors.

Use either inset or overlay doors.

3"–6"

2"–4"

When installing against a wall, use fitting strips (also known as scribing strips). These strips are attached to the cabinet and fitted to variations in the wall profile.

This illustration shows standard measurements for most built-in and freestanding cabinetry. If multiple units are built and installed next to each other, the top and base mouldings are applied last and run the length of all the cabinets to tie them together visually.

Building separate upper and lower cabinets, as well as building no cabinet more than 36" wide, will aid in moving and installing them. If possible, make all shelves adjustable and removable. Also, use clip-on European hinges so the doors can be removed during moving and installation. After installation, the doors are simply clipped back on the cabinets.

This type of cabinet configuration is easily adapted to a small, medium, large or whole-wall entertainment center. By adding different styles of doors, base and top mouldings and hardware, a wide variety of options becomes available.

shelving tips

> > When deciding where shelving will be placed, remember to keep the shelves 36" or less in length. Any longer and the shelves will sag. To add strength to a plywood or particleboard shelf, a $\frac{3}{4}$" × $1\frac{1}{4}$"—$1\frac{1}{2}$" hardwood strip can be attached to the front edge. Also, a shelf can be made of solid hardwood, which is stronger than plywood.

work in a given situation and in what order you need to cut parts and do assemblies.

Only when you are sure of the amount of materials you will need are you ready to go shopping. Take the list with you and double-check it as you gather your materials.

Ready, Set, Cut

At some point you'll need to make that first cut into your carefully chosen materials. Have your cutting list where you can see it, don your safety goggles and let it rip.

As you're cutting out the parts, visualize what it is you're cutting. After you've cut it out, label the part using chalk. Indicate any machining operations (cutting of dadoes, rabbets, grooves, applying edge banding, etc.) that still need to be done to the part at a later time. Write this information on the part. When you've got a sizable pile of parts, it's good to know what's what and where it goes.

If the entertainment center is large and/or has several separate cabinets, be sure they can be moved out of your shop and to the final location without having to remove house doorjambs or a window (yes, this has happened — many times in some cases).

Building knockdown cabinets is sometimes the easiest way to finish and transport the parts. Once they are at the job site, they can be easily re-assembled.

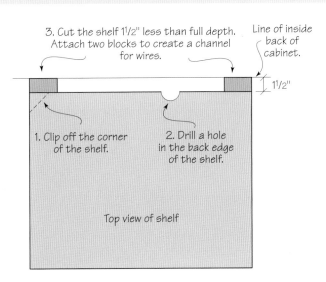

3. Cut the shelf 1½" less than full depth. Attach two blocks to create a channel for wires.

Line of inside back of cabinet.

1½"

1. Clip off the corner of the shelf.

2. Drill a hole in the back edge of the shelf.

Top view of shelf

Three options for creating wire chases between shelves and vertical cabinet dividers.

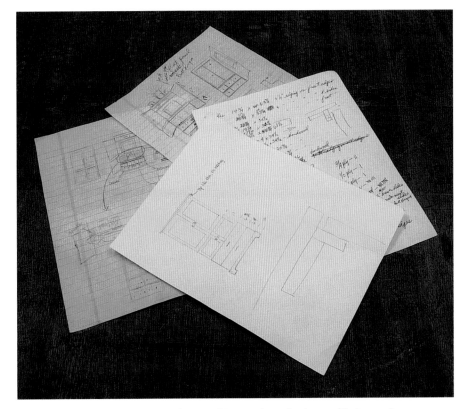

Using a cutting list will save you from making cutting mistakes and help you keep all the parts organized.

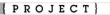

corner
tv cabinet

{ BY JIM STACK }

A corner cabinet can be a good choice if you have a limited amount of space in a room. Putting a television in the corner also makes it viewable from anywhere in the entire room.

This cabinet can be installed in a room and painted the same color as the walls for a seamless look. It is about 19" deep, so the face of the cabinet has the potential for being about 5½' wide if it is built wall-to-wall in a corner. To remedy this situation, it's built with square sides that dive into the corner walls. The top is made to fit into the corner.

The television sits on top of the cabinet, and the components are located inside the cabinet. There is no back, so the wires to the components can be easily fed wherever they need to go. A slot is cut into the cabinet top to create a chase for the wires to the television.

The entire cabinet is made of plywood with the exposed edges covered with veneer tape.

The unit could also be made of top-grade veneers and finished clear. For a small and economical media center, this is the cabinet of choice.

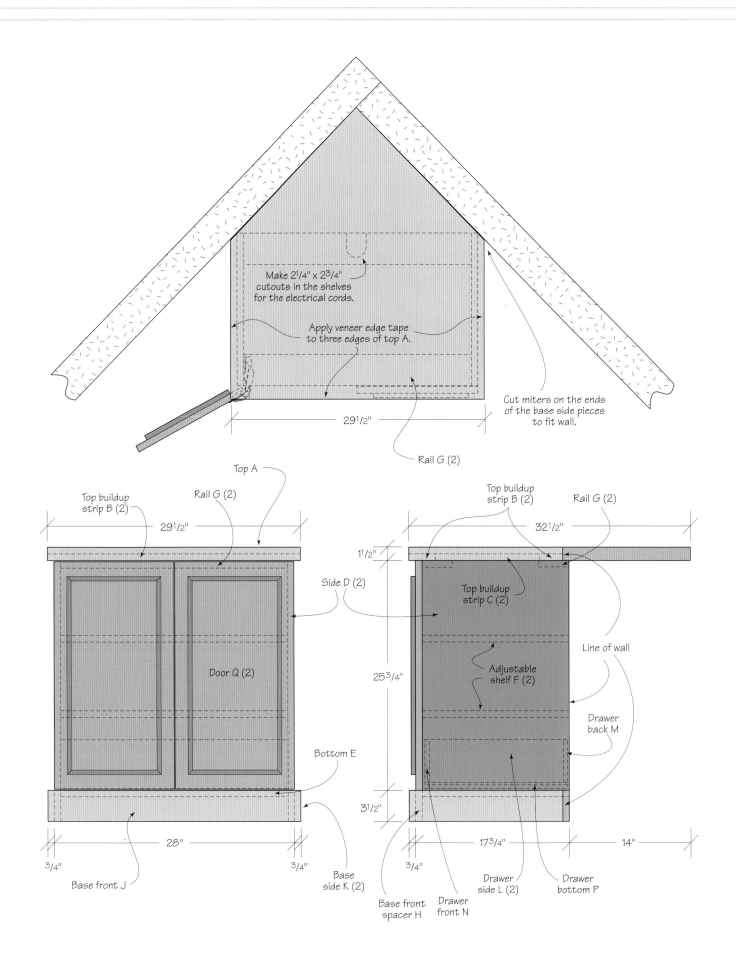

Make 2¹/₄" x 2³/₄" cutouts in the shelves for the electrical cords.

Apply veneer edge tape to three edges of top A.

Cut miters on the ends of the base side pieces to fit wall.

29¹/₂"

Rail G (2)

Top A

Rail G (2)

Top buildup strip B (2)

29¹/₂"

Side D (2)

Door Q (2)

Bottom E

28"

³/₄"

³/₄"

Base front J

Base side K (2)

Top buildup strip B (2)

Rail G (2)

32¹/₂"

1¹/₂"

Top buildup strip C (2)

Adjustable shelf F (2)

Line of wall

Drawer back M

25³/₄"

3¹/₂"

17³/₄"

14"

³/₄"

Base front spacer H

Drawer front N

Drawer side L (2)

Drawer bottom P

inches (millimeters)

REFERENCE	QUANTITY	PART	STOCK	THICKNESS	(mm)	WIDTH	(mm)	LENGTH	(mm)	COMMENTS
A	1	top	plywood	3/4	(19)	29 1/2	(749)	32 1/2	(826)	w/3/4" × 1 1/2" (19mm × 38mm) veneer edge tape on front edge and 2 short side edges
B	2	top buildup strips	plywood	3/4	(19)	3	(76)	29 1/2	(749)	
C	2	top buildup strips	plywood	3/4	(19)	3	(76)	12 1/2	(318)	
D	2	sides	plywood	3/4	(19)	17	(432)	29 1/4	(743)	w/3/4"-wide (19mm-wide) veneer edge tape on front edge of sides
E	1	bottom	plywood	3/4	(19)	17	(432)	26 1/2	(673)	
F	2	adjustable shelves	plywood	3/4	(19)	17	(432)	26 1/2	(673)	w/3/4"-wide (19mm-wide) veneer edge tape on front edge of shelves
G	2	rails	plywood	3/4	(19)	3 1/2	(89)	26 1/2	(673)	w/3/4"-wide (19mm-wide) veneer edge tape on front edge of 1 rail
H	1	base front spacer	plywood	3/4	(19)	3 1/2	(89)	29 1/2	(750)	w/3/4"-wide (19mm-wide) veneer edge tape on top edge
J	1	base front	plywood	3/4	(19)	3 1/2	(89)	29 1/2	(750)	w/3/4"-wide (19mm-wide) veneer edge tape on top edge, 45° bevel on 2 ends
K	2	base sides	plywood	3/4	(19)	3 1/2	(89)	17 3/4	(451)	w/3/4"-wide (19mm-wide) veneer edge tape on top edges, 45° bevel on 2 ends, 1 bevel fit to wall
L	2	drawer sides	plywood	1/2	(13)	5 1/2	(140)	16	(406)	
M	1	drawer back	plywood	1/2	(13)	4 3/4	(121)	24 1/2	(622)	
N	1	drawer front	plywood	1/2	(13)	5 1/2	(140)	26 1/4	(667)	w/3/4"-wide (19mm-wide) veneer edge tape on top edge
P	1	drawer bottom	plywood	1/4	(6)	16 1/4	(413)	22	(559)	
Q	2	doors	plywood	3/4	(19)	13 15/16	(354)	25 1/2	(648)	w/3/4"-wide (19mm-wide) veneer edge tape on all 4 edges of each door

hardware

2 pairs	170°-swing self-closing European hinges
1 set	16" (406mm) full-extension drawer glides
8	5mm shelf pins
12' (4m)	moulding for doors
35' (11m)	3/4"-wide (19mm-wide) veneer edge tape
	1" (25mm) flathead sheet-metal screws
	1 1/2" (38mm) sheet-metal screws
	3/4" (19mm) sheet-metal screws
	3/8"-diameter (10mm-diameter) maple plugs
	stepped dowels
	pin staples
	glue
	spackling compound, primer, paint

1 Lay out the top and cut it to shape. Glue and staple (or attach using screws) the buildup strips to the bottom of the top.

2 Edge-band all the parts that require it. Self-adhesive wood veneer edge tape is the best material to cover the edge grain of plywood.

3 Peel the backing off the tape and stick it to the edges of the plywood. Use a roller or a hardwood block to press the tape securely in place.

4 Trim the edges of the tape with a file and sand smooth.

6 Cut a ¼"-wide by ¼"-deep dado in the drawer sides, ½" up from the bottom. The drawer is assembled using 1" flathead sheet-metal screws.

5 Using stepped dowels, attach the sides to the bottom panel and top rails. After the glue dries, trim the dowels flush with the cabinet and sand smooth. Next, glue the base front spacer to the front edge of the bottom shelf and the lower front edges of the sides. Then, cut the miters on the base front and glue it to the base front spacer. Finally, cut the two base side pieces with miters to fit the base front. Cut the miters on the opposite ends of the base side pieces so they will fit the angle of the corner (see the illustration). Glue the base side pieces to the cabinet sides.

7 Attach the drawer front with 1½" sheet-metal screws countersunk ¼". Plug the screw holes with ⅜"-diameter maple plugs. Cut and sand the plugs flush with the drawer front surface.

8 Slide the drawer bottom into the grooves in the drawer sides and front, and secure it to the bottom of the drawer back with ¾" sheet-metal screws.

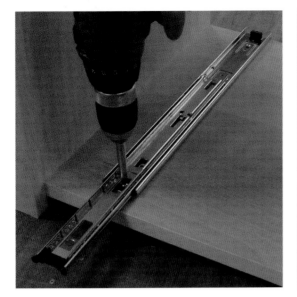

9 Install the drawer glide hardware in the center of the drawer side and locate the cabinet part of the glide on the cabinet side, accordingly.

10 Using glue and pin staples, attach the moulding to the faces of the doors. Adding this moulding is a simple but attractive way to give this cabinet some style.

11 Drill the cup holes for the European hinges according to the instructions included with the hinges. Be sure to double-check the location of the hinges before drilling the cup holes. Remember that the lower hinge on each door will be located *above* the drawer.

12 Using a homemade template, drill the holes for the shelf pins. The shelves will be located between the hinge plates.

installing the corner tv cabinet

>> This project can be put into a corner and left unattached, but it is recommended that it be permanently installed.

Begin by setting the cabinet in place. Scribe the top of the cabinet to the corner wall. Trim the top to the scribe lines and set the cabinet in place. Reach inside the cabinet and draw a line on each wall underneath the top. These lines will give you the locations for two cleats to support the top. Remove the cabinet and, using 3" drywall screws, mount two hardwood cleats ($\frac{3}{4}$" $\times$ $\frac{3}{4}$" $\times$ 16"–20") on the wall immediately under the lines you drew. (It's best if at least one attaching screw can be installed in a wall stud.)

Set the cabinet back in place and install some 1$\frac{1}{4}$" screws from underneath the cabinet, through the cleats and into the bottom of the top. This will secure the cabinet in place.

The room's base trim is cut at a 45° miter and fit to the base of the cabinet.

If a seamless look is wanted, use painter's caulk to fill the gaps where the cabinet meets the wall, and paint to match.

13 Prior to priming the cabinet, use quick-drying spackling compound to fill any gaps. Then, apply a coat of primer and let it dry. Primer has a lot of solids and will build a good base coat that can be sanded smooth. If necessary, apply another coat of primer. Finally, apply a top coat of paint. If you've primed and sanded the primer properly, the top coat will lay down smooth and give good coverage. Apply another top coat if necessary. Reinstall the hardware, hang the doors and attach the door handles.

14 The finished cabinet will have a clean look because all the gaps were filled and primed before the final top coat was applied.

icebox entertainment center

{ BY JIM STUARD }

Before the time came when Americans traded up to an electric fridge, they often kept perishables in an insulated oak box that was cooled by ice. The small versions of these well-built but now useless boxes survived the early 20th century to become TV stands for young couples or impoverished students. Now they fetch $300 to $600 in antique stores, and oak furniture outlet stores sell reproductions for hundreds of dollars.

This is truly a case where you can save some serious dough by building one yourself. This is a great project for beginners, because construction is simple and you don't need a lot of fancy machinery.

A Case For Storage

I used curly oak for this project, which is a difficult species to find. White or red oak will do fine and is available at lumberyards already surfaced, so you don't need a planer. Begin construction by gluing up smaller boards to make the wide panels for the sides, top and shelves. Use biscuits to index the boards' edges. After the glue is dry, remove your panels from the clamps and cut them to the finished size.

Now lay out the $\frac{3}{4}$" $\times$ $\frac{1}{4}$" dadoes in the sides that will hold the shelf and bottom and cut them using a dado stack in your table saw or with a router. Cut a $\frac{1}{4}$"-deep by $\frac{1}{2}$"-wide rabbet on the back edge of the sides to hold the $\frac{1}{4}$" plywood back, as shown in the photo. You'll also need to cut this same

Cut a stopped rabbet in the rear edge of the top for the back. Then cut the $\frac{1}{2}$" $\times$ $\frac{1}{4}$" rabbet in the rear edge of the sides for the back. Do this with a clamped-on straightedge and a router.

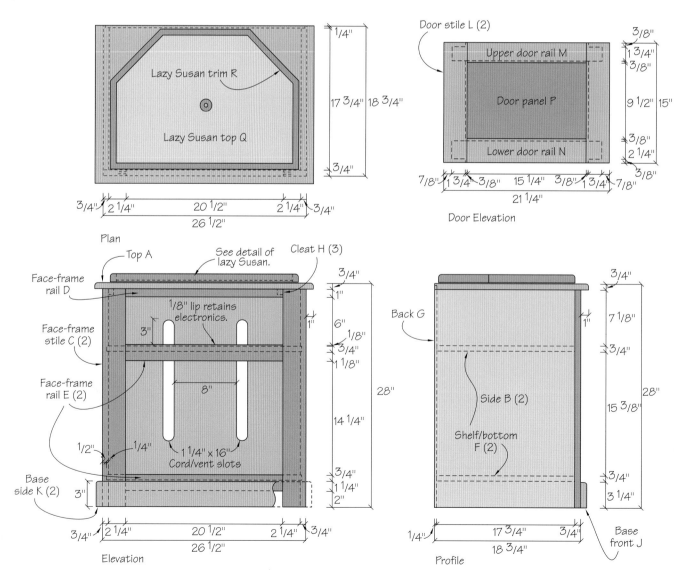

inches (millimeters)

REFERENCE	QUANTITY	PART	STOCK	THICKNESS	(mm)	WIDTH	(mm)	LENGTH	(mm)	COMMENTS
A	1	top	oak	3/4	(19)	19³/4	(502)	28¹/2	(724)	
B	2	sides	oak	3/4	(19)	18	(457)	27¹/4	(692)	
C	2	face-frame stiles	oak	3/4	(19)	3	(76)	27¹/4	(692)	
D	1	face-frame rail	oak	3/4	(19)	1	(25)	22¹/2	(572)	includes tenon length
E	2	face-frame rails	oak	3/4	(19)	2	(51)	22¹/2	(572)	includes tenon length
F	2	shelf/bottom	oak	3/4	(19)	17³/4	(451)	25¹/2	(648)	
G	1	back	oak	1/4	(6)	26	(660)	24¹/2	(623)	
H	3	cleats	oak	3/4	(19)	3/4	(19)	16	(406)	
J	1	base front	oak	3/4	(19)	3	(76)	28	(711)	
K	2	base sides	oak	3/4	(19)	3	(76)	19¹/2	(496)	
L	2	door stiles	oak	3/4	(19)	3	(76)	15	(381)	
M	1	upper door rail	oak	3/4	(19)	2¹/2	(64)	19¹/4	(489)	includes tenon length
N	1	lower door rail	oak	3/4	(19)	3	(76)	19¹/4	(489)	includes tenon length
P	1	door panel	oak	3/4	(19)	15³/4	(400)	10	(254)	
Q	1	lazy Susan top	plywood	3/4	(19)	16	(406)	23	(584)	
R	1	lazy Susan trim	oak	3/4	(19)	1	(25)	96	(2438)	
S	2	laminate discs	HPL	¹/16	(2)	15³/4 d	(400)			
T	1	Masonite disc	hardboard	1/4	(6)	15³/4 d	(400)			

hardware

1 pair	hinges	Van Dyke's Restorers
1	catch	Van Dyke's Restorers
1	nameplate	Van Dyke's Restorers
16	5/16" (8mm) ball bearings	Bearing Distributors, Inc.
	J.E. Moser's Light Sheraton Mahogany water-soluble dye	
	Benjamin Moore Early American stain	
	glue	
	#20 biscuits	
	1¹/4" (32mm) screws	
	1/4"–20 x 2" (6mm–20 x 51mm) roundhead bolt	
	set nut	
	wing nut	

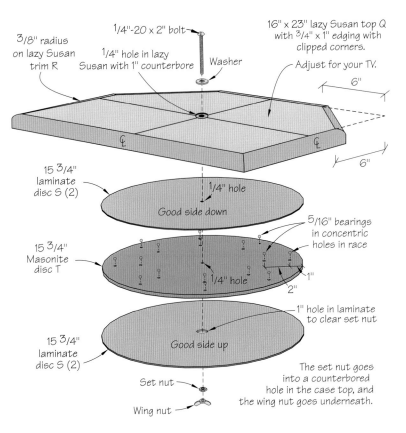

3/8" radius on lazy Susan trim R

1/4"-20 x 2" bolt

1/4" hole in lazy Susan with 1" counterbore

Washer

16" x 23" lazy Susan top Q with 3/4" x 1" edging with clipped corners.

Adjust for your TV.

6"

6"

15 3/4" laminate disc S (2)

1/4" hole

Good side down

5/16" bearings in concentric holes in race

15 3/4" Masonite disc T

1/4" hole

1"

2"

1" hole in laminate to clear set nut

15 3/4" laminate disc S (2)

Good side up

The set nut goes into a counterbored hole in the case top, and the wing nut goes underneath.

Set nut

Wing nut

Start assembling the case by setting a panel on its outer side and setting a shelf into its dado. From underneath, glue and nail into the shelf and side at the corner where the shelf meets the side. Repeat for the other side and check the case for square.

The mortises in the top of the door stiles are $\frac{1}{4}$" x $1\frac{3}{4}$" x $2\frac{1}{8}$" and are $\frac{3}{8}$" down from the end. The mortises in the stile bottoms are $\frac{1}{4}$" x $2\frac{1}{4}$" x $2\frac{1}{8}$", and are $2\frac{1}{8}$" up from the end.

stopped rabbet in the back edge of the top piece. Since your router is set up for this cut, now is a good time.

Glue up your case. Note that the top is attached later with cleats, so don't worry about that now. Glue the shelf and bottom in place in their dadoes and clamp the case together.

A Frame Makes It Stout

Build the face frame using mortise-and-tenon joinery. The face frame consists of two stiles that run from the floor to the top, and three rails that you'll mortise at the dimensions given in the diagram. First lay out the mortises. The mortises are $\frac{1}{4}$" wide, 1" deep and as long as the tenon cut on each rail. Drill out the waste in each mortise with a $\frac{3}{16}$" drill bit and clean up the sides (or cheeks) with a $\frac{1}{4}$" chisel.

Cut the tenons next. All the tenons have a $\frac{1}{4}$" shoulder, except the top of the top rail. Always cut a test joint from scrap before cutting expensive wood. Glue the frame together after you're satisfied with the fit of the joints. Attach the face frame to the case using biscuits and glue. When the

glue is dry, flush up any overhang with a plane and scraper.

Attach the base front with glue and screws. There are biscuit joints cut into the miters and the base sides are glued at the joint but the rest of the side base is attached to the cabinet side with screws inserted in slotted holes drilled in the cabinet sides. This allows for wood movement in the side panels.

Top It Off

The last assembly step on the case is to attach the top and back. For the top piece, I used oak that didn't have a lot of figure, because it is obscured by a rotating lazy Susan.

Attach the top with two cleats that are screwed to the sides and to the top. First, cut your $\frac{3}{4}$" × $\frac{3}{4}$" cleats and drill slotted holes in the cleats to accommodate wood movement. Screw the cleats to the sides and the top to the cleats. Make sure the rabbet in the top lines up with the rabbets in the sides. If everything is square, screw the back to the case.

The Door

The door is frame and panel using haunched mortise-and-tenon joints to join the stiles and rails. The panel is raised on the table saw and floats in a groove in the rails and stiles with the flat side out and the raised side in.

Begin by cutting a $\frac{3}{8}$"-deep by $\frac{1}{4}$"-wide groove for the panel in the stiles and rails. Lay out and cut the mortises in the ends of the stiles and the center of the rails. Cut the $\frac{1}{4}$" by 2"-long tenons on the rails. Then cut a $\frac{3}{8}$" × $1\frac{3}{4}$" notch out of the outside end of each end of the rail, creating the haunch in the tenon. After dry fitting the joints, measure the inside dimensions of the area for the panel. Before gluing the door together, sand the panel. When you're happy with the fit of the door, glue it together, using glue only on the tenons. Keep glue off the panel so it will expand and contract with the seasons.

When the glue is dry, rout a $\frac{3}{8}$" radius on the front edge of the door using a router. Then cut a $\frac{3}{8}$" × $\frac{3}{8}$" rabbet along the back edge of the door. Put a strip of wood that's $\frac{1}{8}$" thick on the front edge of the case bottom. Use this to support the door in its opening on the cabinet. Temporarily attach the cabinet door to the face frame with masking tape. Now mount the hinges on the right side of the door and the catch on the left.

Lazy Susan

This part is optional, but it adds versatility. Most lazy Susans are built for large televisions and are either too clunky or not big enough around to completely support a TV. My home-made lazy Susan can be made to any diameter and supports quite a bit of weight (even me). The part that rotates is the platform. It's simply an oak veneer plywood panel, cut according to the materials list, with curly oak edging. The back corners of the top are clipped so it doesn't bump the wall when rotating. Check the footprint of your TV to make sure it fits. The edging is ¾" × 1", goes all the way around the panel and is mitered at the corners.

The mechanism is a simple sandwich, the center of which is a piece of Masonite with holes drilled to hold ⁵⁄₁₆" ball bearings. It acts as a ball bearing

race. The bearing surface is plastic laminate applied to the top of the cabinet and the bottom of the lazy Susan. A ¼" bolt ties it all together and serves as a pivot point.

First find the center point on the pieces of your lazy Susan and a point 10" back from the front edge of the case top that's centered on the top. With a Forstner bit, drill a 1" hole that's ¼" deep for the bolt head in the plywood top. In the center of that hole, drill a ¼" hole the rest of the way through the top.

Repeat the process on the case's top. These holes will hold a bolt that secures the lazy Susan assembly. To assemble the mechanism, start by placing a ¼"–20 × 2" roundhead bolt with a washer through the plywood top. Place this upside down on a blanket or cardboard. Place the first piece of laminate (colored side away from the top) on the bolt and mark its outline.

Using contact adhesive, attach the laminate to the top, using the bolt as an indexing pin. Attach the laminate to the case top in the same manner, except drill a 1" hole through the laminate to accept a set nut that will secure

the bolt. Because the case top is solid wood, you'll need to attach this laminate by applying the adhesive in a strip oriented with the grain at the center to allow for wood movement.

After attaching the laminate to the case top, drill ⁵⁄₁₆" holes in the Masonite for the ball bearings (ream the holes out a little). Place a set nut on the bolt down to the Masonite. Leave it a little loose so you can lock it down later from underneath the case top with the wing nut.

Finish

The finish on these old refrigerators was fairly light. I wanted to add a little age to my finish and show off the spectacular figure in the curly oak. After finish-sanding the entire cabinet, begin finishing by applying an aniline dye. When this is dry, apply a coat of brown stain to diffuse some of the orange from the dye. Three coats of clear lacquer and a light rubbing out with some steel wool and wax will give this entertainment unit some entertainment value of its own.

Set your table saw to about 12° to cut the bevel on the door panel. Leave a little less than ¼" thickness on the edge of the panel. The panel should be ¹⁄₁₆" from bottoming out in the groove of the door frame.

Put the ball bearings in the holes in the Masonite and place the top onto the assembly. Tie the whole unit together with a washer and wing nut. You should be able to rotate the lazy Susan and not see the bolt move.

standard
media cabinet

{ BY AMY ZIMMER AND JIM STACK }

When Amy, a co-worker, came to me and said she would like to make a media cabinet, I asked her if she knew what she wanted, or if she wanted to start from the very beginning. She said she "sort of" knew, but wanted to know if I had any ideas.

I told her to start by getting the measurements of all the electronic equipment she wanted to put into the cabinet. When she came back the next day with all the dimensions, I knew she was serious, so I gave her some books and magazines that had lots of ideas for media centers.

After looking through all the materials, she came back with some sketches. I was impressed that she had put her ideas on paper. We looked through them and decided to take elements of one idea and put it with another. Eventually we had created a cabinet concept. It fit her needs and was in a style that she liked.

Since she lived in a small apartment, I suggested that she make the cabinet from a light-colored wood so it wouldn't appear too large. She agreed, and then she asked me if I would help her build the cabinet.

I agreed, so the process of creating a materials list, cutting list and hardware list commenced. When we finished, we knew what materials we needed and in what quantities. After trips to the wood store and to the hardware store, we were ready to start making some sawdust.

We spent about two and a half months of lunch hours building the media cabinet. It was a test of patience for us because it's tough to get much done in such short blocks of time. What made it easier was the fact that we had it all on paper and could start right where we left off each time. Sometimes neither of us was available for several days in a row, so it was a good test of how organized we were. We old guys tend to forget what we were doing five minutes ago, so Amy would help me remember what we had been doing the last time we worked.

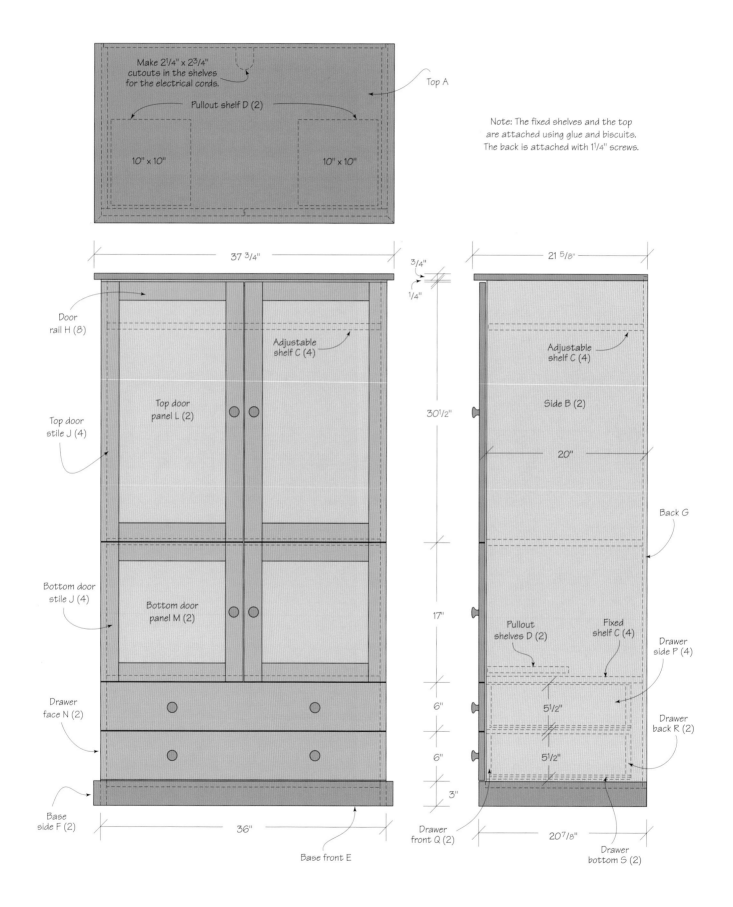

Make 2¼" x 2¾" cutouts in the shelves for the electrical cords.

Pullout shelf D (2)

Top A

10" x 10"

10" x 10"

Note: The fixed shelves and the top are attached using glue and biscuits. The back is attached with 1¼" screws.

37 ¾"

3/4"

1/4"

21 5/8"

Door rail H (8)

Adjustable shelf C (4)

Adjustable shelf C (4)

Top door panel L (2)

Side B (2)

30½"

20"

Top door stile J (4)

Back G

Bottom door stile J (4)

Bottom door panel M (2)

17"

Pullout shelves D (2)

Fixed shelf C (4)

Drawer side P (4)

5½"

Drawer face N (2)

6"

Drawer back R (2)

5½"

6"

Base side F (2)

36"

3"

Base front E

Drawer front Q (2)

20⅞"

Drawer bottom S (2)

inches (millimeters)

REFERENCE	QUANTITY	PART	STOCK	THICKNESS	(mm)	WIDTH	(mm)	LENGTH	(mm)	COMMENTS
A	1	top	plywood	³/₄	(19)	21³/₈	(543)	37¹/₄	(946)	w/¹/₄" × ³/₄" (6mm × 19mm) edging on 1 long and 2 short edges
B	2	sides	plywood	³/₄	(19)	19³/₄	(502)	63³/₄	(1619)	w/¹/₄" × ³/₄" (6mm × 19mm) edging on front edge
C	4	shelves	plywood	³/₄	(19)	19¹/₂	(495)	34¹/₂	(876)	w/¹/₄" × ³/₄" (6mm × 19mm) edging on front edge; 3 fixed and 1 adjustable
D	2	pullout shelves	plywood	³/₄	(19)	10	(254)	10	(254)	w/¹/₄" × ³/₄" (6mm × 19mm) edging on 4 edges
E	1	base front	hardwood	³/₄	(19)	3	(76)	37¹/₂	(953)	45° bevel on 2 ends
F	2	base sides	hardwood	³/₄	(19)	3	(76)	20³/₄	(527)	45° bevel on 1 end
G	1	back	plywood	¹/₂	(13)	35¹/₂	(902)	62	(1575)	
H	8	door rails	hardwood	³/₄	(19)	2¹/₄	(57)	13⁷/₁₆	(341)	
J	4	top door stiles	hardwood	³/₄	(19)	2¹/₄	(57)	30¹/₂	(775)	
K	4	bottom door stiles	hardwood	³/₄	(19)	2¹/₄	(57)	17	(432)	
L	2	top door panels	plywood	¹/₄	(6)	14⁷/₁₆	(367)	27	(686)	
M	2	bottom door panels	plywood	¹/₄	(6)	14⁷/₁₆	(367)	13¹/₂	(343)	
N	2	drawer faces	hardwood	³/₄	(19)	6	(152)	36	(914)	
P	4	drawer sides	hardwood	¹/₂	(13)	5¹/₂	(140)	18	(457)	
Q	2	drawer fronts	hardwood	¹/₂	(13)	5¹/₂	(140)	32¹/₂	(826)	
R	2	drawer backs	hardwood	¹/₂	(13)	4³/₄	(121)	32¹/₂	(826)	
S	2	drawer bottoms	plywood	¹/₄	(6)	17³/₄	(451)	32	(813)	

Note: The ¹/₄" × ³/₄" (6mm × 19mm) edging is made from ¹/₄" × ¹³/₁₆" (6mm × 21mm) hardwood strips and trimmed to fit.

hardware

8	1¹/₄" (32mm)-diameter wooden knobs
2 sets	18" (457mm) full-extension drawer glides
4 sets	18" (457mm) undermount drawer glides
2 pair	pivot hinges
4	magnetic catches
4	5mm shelf pins
	glue
	#20 biscuits
	lacquer

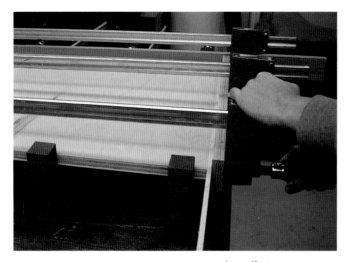

1 After the cabinet parts are cut out, glue ¼" x ¹³⁄₁₆" hardwood strips to the front edges of all the shelves and sides. These strips cover the plywood and provide protection for the edges of the veneer.

2 When the glue has dried, trim the strips flush to the surface of the plywood with a block plane or a router set up with a flush trimming bit. Be careful not to nick the veneer. Sand the joint smooth.

3 Lay out where the fixed shelf will be attached to the sides and cut double slots for #20 biscuits. These double slots provide tremendous holding power for the fixed shelves. Then cut the matching slots in the ends of the shelves.

4 After all the slots are cut, assemble the cabinet. Then, glue the front base onto the cabinet. Next, glue the side base pieces in place. Take your time to cut and fit the miter joints where the front meets the sides.

5 We made a template for the cutout on the front base piece and used it to guide a router with a straight-cutting bit. This step could be done before the base is glued into place, but this seemed easier because the base was already in place and it was easy to make this router setup.

6 After cutting the grooves in the stiles and rails for the doors (make sure the ¼" door panels fit into the grooves!), cut the tenons. We used a dado-cutting setup in the table saw, but using a single blade will work also. Just nibble the material away a little at a time. In either case, set the saw's fence so you will be cutting the full length of the tenon when the end of the rail is against the fence.

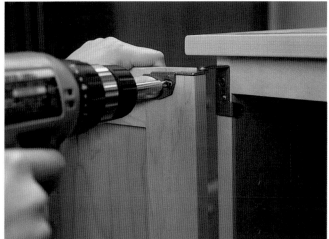

7 When assembling the doors, do it on a flat surface. This will ensure your door will be flat when you glue it together. Always check the door for square by measuring the diagonals. When they are equal, the door is square. If the door isn't square, loosen the clamps and skew them slightly to pull the door square. Assemble the drawers, install the drawer and pullout shelf hardware. Attach the pullout shelves to the hardware following the hardware instructions.

8 We decided to use pivot hinges on the doors. These allow the doors to lie almost flat against the sides of the cabinet when they are open. When the doors are closed, the hinges are hardly noticeable, which fits in with the straight-lined, flat-panel look of the cabinet. This cabinet was finished with three coats of clear lacquer.

rustic

tv cabinet

{ BY JIM STACK }

This TV cabinet is made of yellow pine. The softer parts of the wood have been removed with a wire brush installed in a hand drill. This, plus the use of dark brown and pickling white wood stains, gives the surface of the wood a weathered look. Outdoor strap hinges that have been aged and wooden latches for the doors add to the rustic feel of this cabinet.

The cabinet is made with frame and panel construction. The back and side panels float in the frames. The cabinet's bottom, interior panels and two shelves are plywood, so seasonal wood movement won't be a concern.

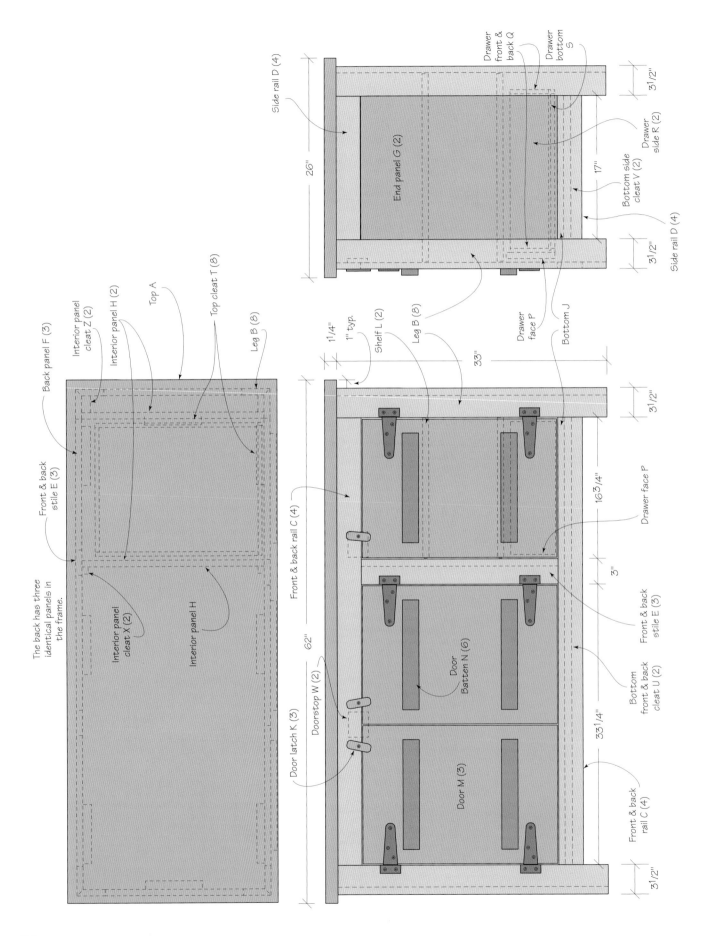

Side rail D (4)

26"

End panel G (2)

Drawer front & back Q

Drawer bottom S

3 1/2"

Drawer side R (2)

Bottom side cleat V (2)

17"

Side rail D (4)

3 1/2"

Back panel F (3)

Interior panel cleat Z (2)

Interior panel H (2)

Top A

Top cleat T (8)

Leg B (8)

Front & back stile E (3)

The back has three identical panels in the frame.

Interior panel cleat X (2)

Interior panel H

Door latch K (3)

Doorstop W (2)

62"

Front & back rail C (4)

1 1/4"

1" typ.

33"

Shelf L (2)

Leg B (8)

3 1/2"

Drawer face P

Bottom J

16 3/4"

3"

Front & back stile E (3)

Bottom front & back cleat U (2)

33 1/4"

Door Batten N (6)

Door M (3)

Front & back rail C (4)

3 1/2"

inches (millimeters)

REFERENCE	QUANTITY	PART	STOCK	THICKNESS	(mm)	WIDTH	(mm)	LENGTH	(mm)	COMMENTS
A	1	top	pine	1¼	(32)	26	(660)	62	(1575)	wire-brush top and all edges
B	8	legs	pine	¾	(19)	3¾	(95)	33	(838)	45° bevel on one long edge; after legs are glued together, wire-brush outside faces & two long outside edges
C	4	front & back rails	pine	¾	(19)	3	(76)	54½	(1384)	wire-brush outside faces
D	4	side rails	pine	¾	(19)	3	(76)	18½	(470)	wire-brush outside faces
E	3	front & back stiles	pine	¾	(19)	3	(76)	25½	(648)	wire-brush outside faces
F	3	back panels	pine	⅝	(16)	16³⁄₁₆	(411)	25½	(648)	wire-brush outside faces
G	2	end panels	pine	⅝	(16)	17½	(445)	25½	(648)	wire-brush outside faces
H	2	interior panels	plywood	¾	(19)	22½	(572)	27	(686)	
J	1	bottom	plywood	¾	(19)	22½	(572)	58½	(1486)	
K	3	door latches	pine	¼	(6)	1	(25)	3	(76)	wire-brush outside faces and all edges
L	2	shelves	plywood	¾	(19)	16¾	(425)	22¼	(565)	dimensions include two ¾" × 2" × 3" (19mm × 51mm × 76) blocks glued to back edge of shelf
M	3	doors	pine	¾	(19)	16½+/-	(419)	23¾	(603)	fit doors to cabinet openings; wire-brush outside faces & all edges
N	6	door battens	pine	¾	(19)	2	(51)	13	(330)	wire-brush outside faces and all edges
P	1	drawer face	pine	¾	(19)	6	(152)	16³⁄₈	(416)	
Q	2	drawer front & back	plywood	½	(13)	5½	(140)	15½	(394)	
R	2	drawer sides	pine	½	(13)	5½	(140)	19½	(495)	
S	1	drawer bottom	plywood	½	(13)	15½	(394)	20	(508)	
T	8	top cleats	poplar	⅞	(22)	⅞	(22)	7	(178)	
U	2	bottom front & back cleats	poplar	⅞	(22)	⅞	(22)	58½	(1486)	
V	2	bottom side cleats	poplar	⅞	(22)	⅞	(22)	20¾	(527)	
W	2	doorstops	pine	½	(13)	2½	(64)	3	(76)	
X	2	interior panel cleats	pine	⅞	(22)	⅞	(22)	27	(686)	
Y	2	edge strips	pine	¼	(6)	¾	(19)	22¼	(565)	
Z	2	interior panel cleats	pine	⅞	(22)	1	(25)	2	(51)	

hardware

3	pairs	3" (76mm) T-hinges
1	set	20" (508mm) full-extension drawer glides
8		¼" × 1¼" (6mm × 32mm) wooden dowels (used as shelf pins)
		clear packing tape
		glue
		1" (25mm) and 1¼" (32mm) drywall screws
		staples
3		1" (25mm) roundhead screws
		Minwax Pickled Oak #260
		Minwax Dark Walnut #2716

1 Cut out the leg blanks first. Then set the bevel on the table blade to 45° and cut a bevel on one long edge of each leg piece.

2 Lay out two legs pieces faceup with the long beveled edges touching. Tape this joint together with clear packaging tape. (See the sidebar "Taping a Miter Joint" later in the chapter.) You will make four of these assemblies.

3 Cut out all the rails and stiles. Set up a 3/8"-wide dado cutter in your table saw. Cut all the grooves in the legs, stiles and rails. To make it easier to cut the tenons, center the groove cuts in these parts. All the grooves that will show on the front legs, front stile and at the bottoms of all the legs below the bottom rails can be fitted with strips of wood after the cabinet is assembled. I found it easier to run the grooves through all the parts rather than try to make stopped cuts.

4 Cut the rails and front and back stiles to length. Then, cut the tenons on each of these parts. If you centered the groove cuts, cutting the tenons is simply a matter of resetting the table saw fence and the cutter height. When removing the material for the tenons, make the first cut on the end of the rail. Then slide the rail end against the fence as shown to make the second cut. Turn the part over and remove the material to complete the tenon. Remember to make test cuts in scraps of wood first when setting up to cut the tenons.

5 Cut the back, end and interior panels to size. Note that the panels are cut full-length to fit in the frames, but they are cut narrower than full-size. This will allow the panels to move with the changes of seasons. Cut a tenon on the panels to fit into the grooves in the rails, stiles and legs. These tenons should fit easily and smoothly into the grooves. The tenon shoulder will be installed to the inside of the cabinet.

6 Before assembling the cabinet frames, use a wire wheel brush in a drill to texture the pine. In my part of the United States, yellow pine is the wood of choice for this procedure. If you live in other parts of the United States or other countries, other species of pine such as spruce or cedar will work, also. The idea is to remove some of the soft summer growth and leave the harder winter growth intact.

7 The wire-brush texturing leaves a surface like a weathered barn or fence. After staining and finishing, the texturing will become more visible.

8 Assemble the front and back panels first. The legs become the end stiles of these assemblies. Double-check the frames with a framing square or measure the frames from diagonal to diagonal to be sure they're square.

10 Using glue and screws, install the bottom front, back and side cleats.

9 The end panels are assembled at the same time. When the legs are part of the framework, the cabinet casework comes together quickly.

11 Cut the plywood bottom to size and install it so it rests on the cleats inside the cabinet. Attach it with screws inserted into the cleats.

12 Cut the interior panels to size. Then, drill a 2"-diameter or larger hole in the interior panel that separates the television section from the shelf and drawer section of the cabinet. You can make the hole a little larger by cutting away the waste to the back edge of the panel.

13 Using staples or screws, install the interior panel cleats for both interior panels.

14 Drill holes in the interior panels. Using screws, install the interior panels against the cleats.

15 Drill the holes for the shelf pins using a homemade drilling jig. Using a ¹/₄"-thick piece of scrap plywood, make the jig by drilling a straight line of holes 1¹/₂" apart. Place the bottom of the jig on the bottom of the cabinet and hold it firmly against the side of the cabinet. Start and stop the line of holes 6" from the bottom and top of the side of the cabinet. Use a stop on the drill so you won't drill through the cabinet side.

16 Cut the shelves to width and 2" shorter than their finished length. Then, cut four 2" × 3" plywood blocks and glue them to the back edges of the shelves. If you like, you can use biscuits to help glue these blocks in place. Glue solid-wood strips to the front edges of the shelves at the same time. Use a scrap of wood to even out the clamping pressure on the wood strips.

17 Plane the edges of the wood strips on the shelves flush to the top and bottom surfaces of the shelves.

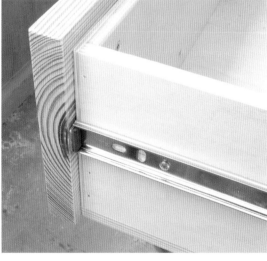

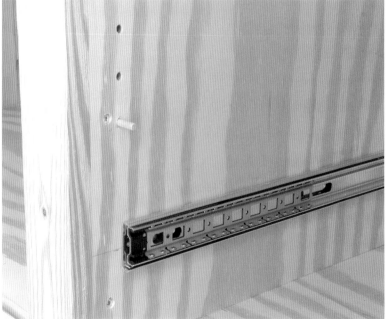

18 Cut the drawer parts to size. Cut a rabbet in the ends of the front and back drawer parts. Attach the sides to the front and back with glue and staples. Then, using glue and screws, attach the drawer bottom to the bottom edges of the drawer box. Center the drawer face on the drawer box. Locate the bottom of the face flush with the bottom of the drawer box and attach it to the drawer box using 1"- drywall screws. Finally, attach the drawer glides to the sides of the drawer box, locating them about halfway up from the bottom of the box.

19 Measure from the bottom of the drawer box to the center of the hardware you attached to the drawer box. Add $\frac{1}{4}$" to this measurement. Use this measurement to measure up from the bottom of the cabinet. Draw a line parallel to the cabinet bottom on the interior panels. Center the cabinet part of the drawer glides on this line and screw the hardware in place. When the drawer is installed, the bottom of the drawer should ride $\frac{1}{4}$" above the bottom of the cabinet.

making hardware rustic

>> Unplated hardware works best when your goal is a rustic look. If plated hardware is what you have, simply sand or scrape off the plating. Put the hardware in a plastic or glass container and cover it with vinegar. This will rust the hardware and give it a nice patina. The process can take from several days to a week or two.

For brass hardware, pour about $\frac{1}{2}$" of ammonia into a container. Remove the plating from the hardware and suspend it on a screen hung inside the container. The hardware should not actually touch the ammonia. The fumes will turn the brass all kinds of colors and give it a great-looking patina. This process takes no more than a few hours. Keep the containers outside or in a well-ventilated area.

Steel hardware can be easily aged by dipping it in gun blue (available at most gun stores) for a minute or two. Brass hardware also can be aged using this chemical. First, remove the lacquer from the hardware with lacquer thinner, by sanding, or both. Dip the hardware in gun blue, remove it when black, and then coat the hardware with lacquer.

20 Make the door panels and cut them to the finished height. Allow approximately a $\frac{1}{8}$" gap at the top and the bottom of the door's opening. Cut the door battens to size and locate them in the center of the doors. Attach them to the doors using screws from the inside of the doors. Drill oversize holes for the screws so they can move with the doors. Do not use any glue to install the battens. Install the hardware on the doors and hang them. Note that the hinges are mounted so the hinge barrel is located on the cabinet frame. This ensures that the hinge won't be sticking out when the door is opened. I know what you're thinking: Why didn't we cut the doors to finished width? We'll let the doors hang on the cabinet for about a week, then come back and fit them to the door's openings. Construction lumber is usually high in moisture content (up to 20 percent). After the lumber is machined, the pine will shrink, warp and cup while the doors are hanging. This wood movement is part of the rustic style. After a week, fit the doors. Remove the battens and hinges. Texture the door faces and edges. Texture the battens and reattach them to the doors. Hang the doors and install the doorstops on the inside of the top rail as shown in the illustration.

21 Cut the door latches, texture and install them with one roundhead screw each.

finishing tips for a textured wood surface

>> The stain for this project is a 50/50 mixture of Pickled Oak #260 and Dark Walnut #2716 made by Minwax. The dark stain is the basic color, but by adding the white pickling stain, a gray cast is added to the wood, giving it the weathered look of an old barn.

Apply the stain with a bristle brush, let it soak into the textured wood and dry overnight. Don't rub any of the stain off the wood. Any rag used to rub the stain off would leave lots of cloth fibers stuck on the rough surface of the wood, and the stain looks good just the way it is!

Top-coat with a flat-sheen polyurethane finish. Apply this top coat to the inside of the cabinet as well as the outside, using a brush or spraying it. If you spray, be sure you apply a wet coat. If the sprayed coat is a mist coat that isn't totally wet, the rough fibers of the textured wood will look like they have frost on them. You'll need to sand this off, which will start smoothing the textured wood, and you don't want to do that.

22 After you've completed final assembly and all the doors, shelves and drawers fit, it's time to prep the project for finishing. Not a lot needs to be done to this piece because of the texture of the wood. Using a sanding block and some 100-grit sandpaper, soften the sharp edges of the cabinet and doors. Sand the flat surfaces by sanding with the grain. All you want to do is knock off some of the strings of wood fibers.

23 Here's how the wood finish and aged hardware look. Building this style of furniture is fun and involves some out-of-the-ordinary techniques you might like to try.

taping a miter joint

>> One of the easiest and quickest ways to glue a miter joint is to tape it with clear packaging tape. Even those tricky compound miter joints are child's play using this technique.

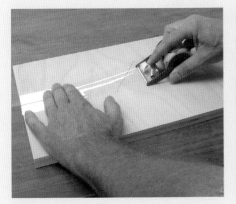

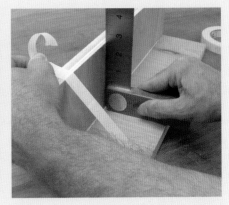

STEP 1 After the miters have been cut on the parts, lay the parts faceup so the sharp, mitered edges are touching. (When doing this with plywood, it is possible to cut the parts so the grain pattern will continue through the joint.) Then, tape the joint with clear packaging tape. Use a smooth block of wood or a roller to press the tape firmly on the wood.

STEP 2 Turn the assembly facedown. Apply a thin, smooth layer of glue to both mitered edges. Don't use too much glue; the pressure created when the assembly is folded could force the joint apart.

STEP 3 Fold the assembly and use masking tape or a clamp to hold it square until the glue sets.

STEP 4 To glue compound miter-cut parts together, lay them out as shown. Tape each joint, flip the assembly facedown and apply the glue to the joints.

STEP 5 Fold the box into shape, hold the final joint together and tape it.

ash armoire media center

{ BY JIM STACK }

One of the great features of this project is that it can be knocked down into smaller parts. Add a hanging rail in the top section and this cabinet can be used as an armoire. It has as much space as a small closet. It can also be used as a media center, complete with a shelf large enough to hold two or three video components. The drawers can be fitted with CD, DVD or VCR-tape organizers. The back has a removable panel for easy access to all the electronic components. The panels in the doors and sides are resawn and bookmatched. I picked wood with lots of colors and figured grain patterns for these panels and used the straighter-grained pieces for the rails, stiles and legs. The finish is clear lacquer.

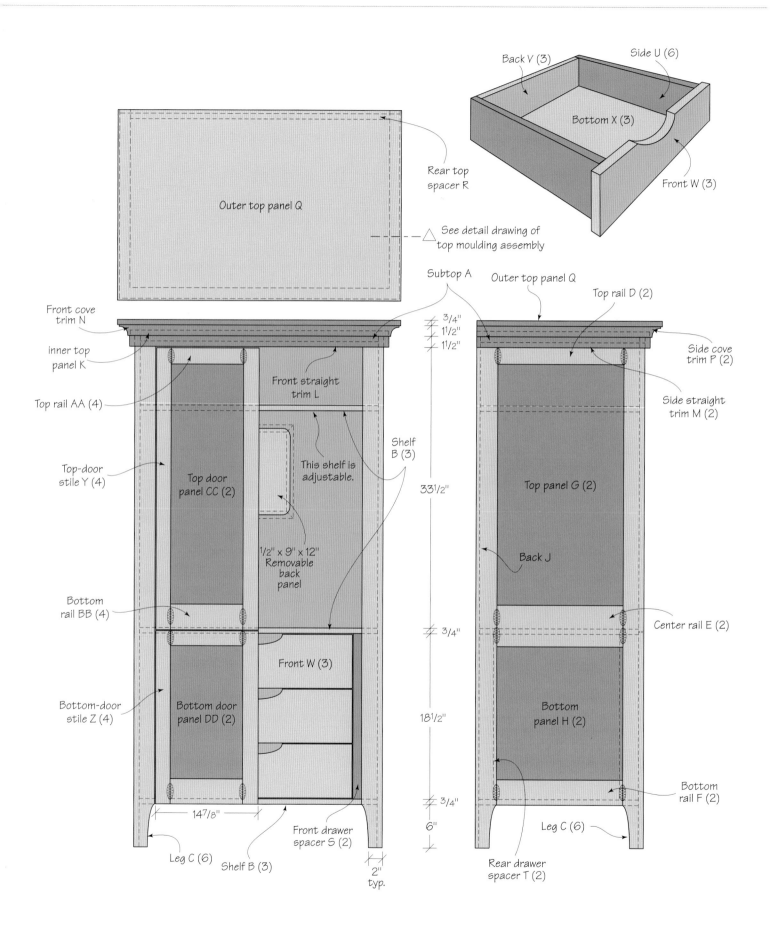

Back V (3)

Side U (6)

Bottom X (3)

Front W (3)

Rear top spacer R

Outer top panel Q

△ See detail drawing of top moulding assembly

Subtop A

Outer top panel Q

Top rail D (2)

Front cove trim N

inner top panel K

Top rail AA (4)

Top-door stile Y (4)

Top door panel CC (2)

Front straight trim L

Shelf B (3)

This shelf is adjustable.

Side cove trim P (2)

Side straight trim M (2)

Top panel G (2)

3/4"
1 1/2"
1 1/2"

33 1/2"

1/2" x 9" x 12" Removable back panel

Bottom rail BB (4)

Back J

Bottom-door stile Z (4)

Bottom door panel DD (2)

Front W (3)

Bottom panel H (2)

Center rail E (2)

3/4"

18 1/2"

14 7/8"

Front drawer spacer S (2)

Leg C (6)   Shelf B (3)

2" typ.

Rear drawer spacer T (2)

Bottom rail F (2)

Leg C (6)

3/4"

6"

48

inches (millimeters)

REFERENCE	QUANTITY	PART	STOCK	THICKNESS	(mm)	WIDTH	(mm)	LENGTH	(mm)	COMMENTS
CASE										
A	1	subtop	birch plywood	$^3/_4$	(19)	$23^1/_2$	(597)	$34^1/_2$	(877)	two $^3/_4$" × $^3/_4$" (19mm × 19mm) notches for legs
B	3	shelves	birch plywood	$^3/_4$	(19)	$22^3/_4$	(578)	$34^1/_2$	(877)	dimensions include $^1/_4$" × $^3/_4$" (6mm × 19mm) ash strip on shelf front
C	6	legs	ash	$^{13}/_{16}$	(21)	3	(76)	71	(1803)	$^1/_4$" × $^1/_2$" (6mm × 13mm) groove for panels
D	2	top rails	ash	$^{13}/_{16}$	(21)	$3^3/_4$	(95)	18	(457)	$^1/_4$" × $^1/_2$" (6mm × 13mm) groove for panels
E	2	center rails	ash	$^{13}/_{16}$	(21)	$5^3/_4$	(146)	18	(457)	two $^1/_4$" × $^1/_2$" (6mm × 13mm) grooves for panels
F	2	bottom rails	ash	$^{13}/_{16}$	(21)	$3^1/_2$	(89)	18	(457)	$^1/_4$" × $^1/_2$" (6mm × 13mm) groove for panels
G	2	top panels	ash	$^1/_4$	(6)	$18^3/_4$	(476)	$34^1/_2$	(876)	
H	2	bottom panels	ash	$^1/_4$	(6)	$18^3/_4$	(476)	$19^1/_2$	(495)	
J	1	back	birch plywood	$^1/_2$	(13)	$35^1/_2$	(902)	65	(1651)	
TOP MOULDING ASSEMBLY										
K	1	inner top panel	birch plywood	$^3/_4$	(19)	$24^{11}/_{16}$	(628)	$37^3/_8$	(950)	
L	1	front straight trim	ash	$^3/_4$	(19)	$1^1/_2$	(38)	$37^1/_2$	(953)	attached to underside of inner top panel, leaving a $^1/_{16}$" (2mm) lip
M	2	side straight trim	ash	$^3/_4$	(19)	$1^1/_2$	(38)	$24^3/_4$	(629)	attached to underside of inner top panel, leaving a $^1/_{16}$" (2mm) lip
N	1	front cove trim	ash	$1^1/_2$	(38)	$1^1/_2$	(38)	$40^1/_2$	(1029)	attached to front edge of inner top panel, rests on $^1/_{16}$" (2mm) lip
P	2	side cove trim	ash	$1^1/_2$	(38)	$1^1/_2$	(38)	$26^1/_4$	(666)	attached to side edges of inner top panel, rests on $^1/_{16}$" (2mm) lip
Q	1	outer top panel	birch plywood	$^3/_4$	(19)	$26^1/_2$	(673)	41	(1041)	includes $^3/_8$"-thick (10mm-thick) ash strips on front and side edges
R	1	rear top spacer	birch plywood	$^3/_4$	(19)	$^3/_4$	(19)	$37^3/_8$	(950)	attached to top side of inner top panel at back of panel
DRAWERS										
S	2	front drawer spacers	ash	2	(51)	$3^1/_2$	(89)	23	(584)	allows the drawer slides to clear the legs
T	2	rear drawer spacers	soft maple	$1^1/_2$	(38)	$3^1/_2$	(89)	23	(584)	allows the drawer slides to clear the legs
U	6	sides	soft maple	$^1/_2$	(13)	$7^1/_2$	(192)	20	(508)	$^1/_4$" × $^1/_4$" (6mm × 6mm) groove for drawer bottom
V	3	backs	soft maple	$^1/_2$	(13)	$6^1/_4$	(158)	$25^1/_2$	(648)	
W	3	fronts	ash	$^3/_4$	(19)	$7^1/_2$	(192)	$27^3/_8$	(696)	$^1/_4$" × $^1/_4$" (6mm × 6mm) groove for drawer bottom
X	3	bottoms	luan plywood	$^1/_4$	(6)	$20^1/_4$	(514)	26	(660)	
DOORS										
Y	4	top-door stiles	ash	$^{13}/_{16}$	(21)	$2^1/_4$	(57)	$39^1/_4$	(997)	$^1/_4$" × $^1/_2$" (6mm × 13mm) groove for panel
Z	4	bottom-door stiles	ash	$^{13}/_{16}$	(21)	$2^1/_4$	(57)	$24^1/_8$	(613)	$^1/_4$" × $^1/_2$" (6mm × 13mm) groove for panel
AA	4	top rails	ash	$^{13}/_{16}$	(21)	$2^1/_4$	(57)	$10^3/_8$	(264)	$^1/_4$" × $^1/_2$" (6mm × 13mm) groove for panel
BB	4	bottom rails	ash	$^{13}/_{16}$	(21)	$3^1/_2$	(89)	$10^3/_8$	(264)	$^1/_4$" × $^1/_2$" (6mm × 13mm) groove for panel
CC	2	top-door panels	ash	$^1/_4$	(6)	$11^1/_8$	(282)	$34^1/_2$	(876)	
DD	2	bottom-door panels	ash	$^1/_4$	(6)	$11^1/_8$	(282)	$20^5/_8$	(524)	

hardware

36	knockdown hardware inserts
4 pairs	duplex hinges
3 sets	20" (508mm) full-extension drawer glides
4	1" (25mm) wooden pulls
	two-part epoxy
	glue
	#20 biscuits
	$1^1/_4$" (32mm) drywall screws
2	magnetic catches

1 Using a scrap piece of plywood, make a template of the curve at the feet using the dimensions in the illustration to mark the start and end of the curved line. Connect the dots with a curve that looks good to you. Use the template as a guide to trace the pattern onto the feet. Rough-cut the waste material away using a jigsaw.

2 Use the template as a guide and rout the curves smooth.

3 Cut the miters on the two front-leg assemblies, tape the joint and apply glue. (See the sidebar "Taping a Miter Joint" in the previous chapter.)

4 Fold the leg assembly. Use hand screws to hold the assembly square while the glue sets.

5 Here is another method that works well for holding the assembly square.

6 Cut the stopped dadoes for the resawn panels in the legs using a ¼" straight router bit. Cut the biscuit slots for the leg and rail joints. Sand the ¼" panels before assembling the sides. As always, get all the clamps, glue, biscuits and an assistant (if you need one) together before you start assembling.

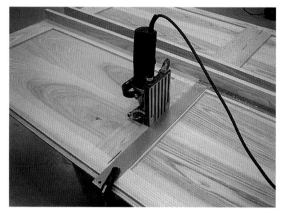

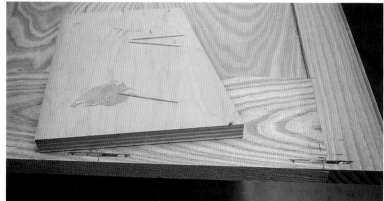

7 Use a carpenter's square as a guide for cutting the slots for the knockdown hardware inserts. Then cut the slots in the ends of the bottom, the middle and the top shelves for the matching knockdown hardware.

8 You will need to use a two-part epoxy for gluing the aluminum hardware into the No. 20–size slots. I mixed a batch of epoxy about the size of a 50-cent piece (remember those?), which was enough to glue five or six pieces of hardware into the slots. I used toothpicks to put the epoxy into the bottom and halfway up the sides of the slots. Don't use too much epoxy or it will get into the inside of the hook on the knockdown hardware and on the top sides of the slot. This makes it impossible to put the two parts together after the epoxy has cured. I recommend practicing putting the epoxy into the slots in scrap material before starting on the project.

9 Make the top frame. (You could also use a solid piece of plywood.) Then glue the straight part of the top moulding onto the frame, letting the moulding hang over the frame about $1/16$". This lip will make it easier to align the cove part of the moulding.

10 I made the cove moulding on the table saw. This has become a common operation, and it is safe if you do it correctly. It works best if you use a sharp, carbide-tooth blade. Before you set up for the cove making, cut a flat face on the moulding material as shown on the piece in the left of the photo above. Set up a fence behind the blade at about a 45° angle to the blade. Clamp it in place and raise the saw blade about $1/8$". Test the cut until it is centered in the moulding material and the cove is the proper radius. (To center the cut, move the fence toward or away from the blade, keeping the angle the same. To change the radius, change the angle of the fence.) Make your first cut in all the moulding pieces. Raise the blade another $1/8$" (or a little less if your saw sounds like it's working too hard). Continue until the cove depth is to your liking. You will probably need to move the fence slightly toward or away from the blade to keep the cut centered, but try not to change the angle of the fence.

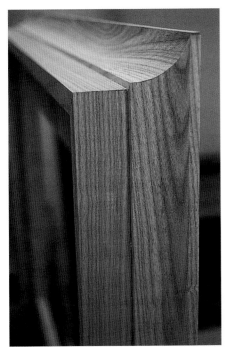

12 Make the long cut for the notches in the top shelf of the cabinet. These notches will clear the front leg stiles and let the front edge of the shelf come flush to the front legs.

13 Make the short cut in two passes.

11 Attach the cove moulding to the top frame by holding it against the lip you created with the straight moulding. You can use small brads or nails to attach the moulding. I chose to clamp it in place to avoid nail holes. Then glue the outer top panel to the top of the top moulding assembly.

Detail of Top Moulding Assembly

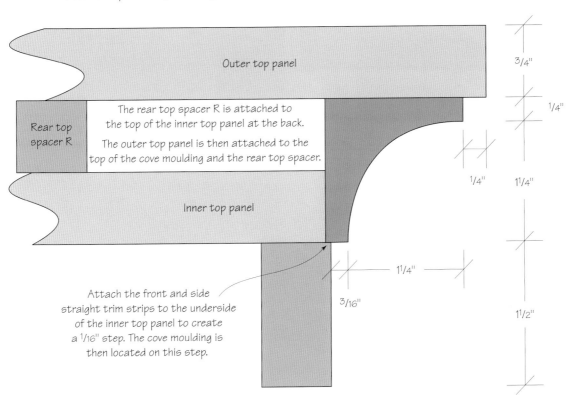

Outer top panel

Rear top spacer R

The rear top spacer R is attached to the top of the inner top panel at the back.

The outer top panel is then attached to the top of the cove moulding and the rear top spacer.

Inner top panel

3/4"

1/4"

1/4"   1¼"

1¼"

3/16"

1½"

Attach the front and side straight trim strips to the underside of the inner top panel to create a 1/16" step. The cove moulding is then located on this step.

14 The drawers are made of soft maple with ash fronts. Use a paint can to draw the curve for the hand cutout on the drawer fronts. Make the cutout with a jigsaw and sand smooth.

15 These drawers use full-extension hardware, so the fronts need to have a ⁷/₁₆" lip extending past both sides. This lip will conceal the hardware when the drawer is closed. The back of the drawer is captured between the sides. Note the spacer to help keep the assembly square.

16 The sides butt into the front.

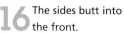

18 Lay out where the hardware will be mounted on the drawers and transfer this to the cabinet sides. Use temporary spacers to hold the hardware parallel to the cabinet bottom. The spacers also ensure the hardware will be located at the same height on both sides of the cabinet.

17 Install the front and rear drawer spacers on each side of the cabinet.

20 I used a ¼" wing cutter in the router to cut the stopped dadoes for the door panel. (A ¼" straight bit will work as well.)

19 Making the drawer fronts out of ash gives the cabinet a more formal furniture look. The hardware on the drawers will last for years of openings and closings.

21 This is what the door frame joints look like before assembly. It is a quick and simple way to make frames (with or without panels).

22 The hinges for this cabinet are duplex and can be mortised with the biscuit joiner. For this project, I added an auxiliary fence to the biscuit joiner because the cabinet face is 3" wide and the fence on the tool wouldn't extend that far. Fit the doors with the spacings you want and set the biscuit joiner to cut a No. 20 slot. Center the cutter on the door and cabinet spacing. Then cut the mortise. You will have a mortise cut into both the door and the cabinet side at the same time. (If you prefer, set the cutter to make the entire mortise in the door.)

23 Above is a detail of the mortise and hinge.

24 The adjustable shelf needs clearance at the back edge for cables and wires. This is an easy way to create that space. Rip 2" off the back side of the adjustable shelf, then glue two wings to the back of the shelf at both ends. (Use biscuits to hold these wings in place, of course.)

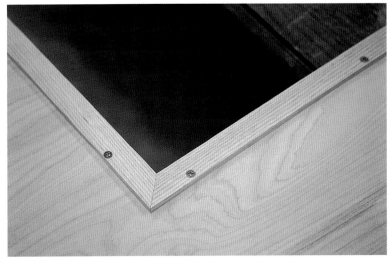

25 Cut out an opening in the upper part of the back panel for cable and wire access. Using ¼"-thick by 1"-wide ash strips, put a frame around the inside edges of the opening to create a ½" lip.

27 Use small magnetic catches to hold the doors closed. These are mounted so that both the top and bottom doors use the same magnet; the top door overlays the top half of each magnet, while the bottom door overlays the bottom half of each magnet.

26 Cut a ½"-thick panel to fit into the cutout from the back of the cabinet, round the corners to match the cutout and attach it with screws.

dresser with

{ BY RICK WILLIAMS }

Most of today's bedrooms either have room for a large dresser or room for a television cabinet — but not both. With this unique project, you get the best of both worlds.

This is a surprisingly easy piece to build because of its three-piece sectional design. It has six large dresser drawers in the base cabinet, and the upper left linen portion has a place for a VCR or DVD unit, as well as room for sweaters and bedspreads.

The upper right portion easily conceals a 19" television behind tambour doors. You'll really appreciate the storage and the organization that exists in this piece of furniture.

television cabinet

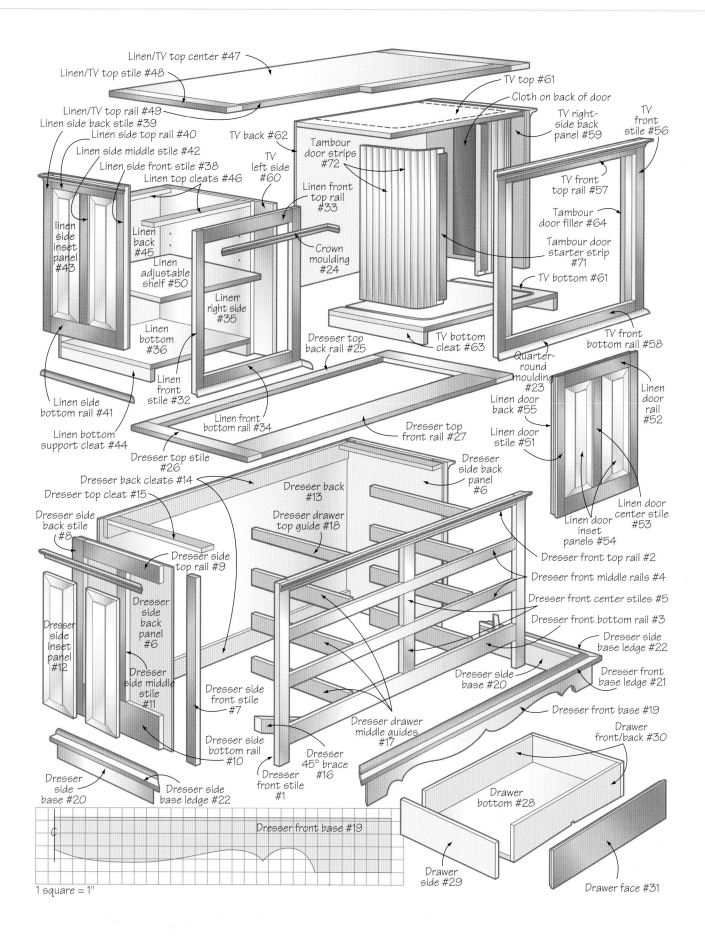

Linen/TV top center #47

Linen/TV top stile #48

Linen/TV top rail #49

Linen side back stile #39

Linen side top rail #40

Linen side middle stile #42

Linen side front stile #38

Linen top cleats #46

TV back #62

TV left side #60

Tambour door strips #72

Linen front top rail #33

TV top #61

Cloth on back of door

TV right-side back panel #59

TV front stile #56

TV front top rail #57

Tambour door filler #64

Tambour door starter strip #71

TV bottom #61

linen side inset panel #43

Linen back #45

Linen adjustable shelf #50

Crown moulding #24

Linen right side #35

Linen bottom #36

Linen front stile #32

Dresser top back rail #25

TV bottom cleat #63

TV front bottom rail #58

Quarter-round moulding #23

Linen door back #55

Linen door stile #51

Linen door rail #52

Linen side bottom rail #41

Linen bottom support cleat #44

Dresser top stile #26

Linen front bottom rail #34

Dresser top front rail #27

Dresser side back panel #6

Linen door center stile #53

Linen door inset panels #54

Dresser back cleats #14

Dresser top cleat #15

Dresser back #13

Dresser drawer top guide #18

Dresser front top rail #2

Dresser side back stile #8

Dresser side top rail #9

Dresser front middle rails #4

Dresser front center stiles #5

Dresser front bottom rail #3

Dresser side base ledge #22

Dresser side inset panel #12

Dresser side back panel #6

Dresser side middle stile #11

Dresser side front stile #7

Dresser drawer middle guides #17

Dresser side base #20

Dresser front base ledge #21

Dresser front base #19

Dresser side base #20

Dresser side bottom rail #10

Dresser front stile #1

Dresser 45° brace #16

Drawer front/back #30

Dresser side base ledge #22

Drawer bottom #28

Drawer side #29

Dresser front base #19

1 square = 1"

Drawer side #29

Drawer face #31

inches (millimeters)

REFERENCE	QUANTITY	PART	STOCK	THICKNESS	(mm)	WIDTH	(mm)	LENGTH	(mm)	COMMENTS
1	2	dresser front stiles	oak	3/4	(19)	1 1/2	(38)	32	(813)	
2	1	dresser front top rail	oak	3/4	(19)	2 3/4	(70)	49	(1245)	
3	1	dresser front bottom rail	oak	3/4	(19)	3 1/2	(89)	49	(1245)	
4	2	dresser front middle rails	oak	3/4	(19)	2	(51)	49	(1245)	
5	3	dresser front center stiles	oak	3/4	(19)	2	(51)	6	(152)	
6	2	dresser side back panels	plywood	1/4	(6)	20 1/4	(514)	32	(813)	
7	2	dresser side front stiles	oak	3/4	(19)	1 1/4	(32)	32	(813)	
8	2	dresser side back stiles	oak	3/4	(19)	2	(51)	32	(813)	
9	2	dresser side top rails	oak	3/4	(19)	2 3/4	(70)	17	(432)	
10	2	dresser side bottom rails	oak	3/4	(19)	7	(178)	17	(432)	
11	2	dresser side middle stiles	oak	3/4	(19)	2	(51)	22 1/4	(565)	
12	4	dresser side inset panels	oak	3/4	(19)	7 1/2	(191)	22 1/4	(565)	
13	1	dresser back	plywood	1/4	(6)	32	(813)	51 1/4	(1301)	
14	2	dresser back cleats	poplar	3/4	(19)	3 1/2	(89)	50	(1270)	
15	2	dresser top cleats	poplar	3/4	(19)	2	(51)	19 1/4	(489)	
16	2	dresser 45° braces	poplar	3/4	(19)	2	(51)	8	(203)	
17	6	dresser drawer middle gds	poplar	3/4	(19)	2 3/8	(61)	20	(508)	
18	2	dresser drawer top guides	poplar	3/4	(19)	2 3/4	(70)	19 1/4	(489)	
19	1	dresser front base	oak	3/4	(19)	4 1/4	(108)	55	(1397)	cut to length on 45°; cut to design
20	2	dresser side bases	oak	3/4	(19)	4 1/4	(108)	23	(584)	cut to length on 45°
21	1	dresser front base ledge	oak	3/4	(19)	1 1/4	(32)	55	(1397)	
22	2	dresser side base ledges	oak	3/4	(19)	1 1/4	(32)	23	(584)	
23	2	quarter-round moulding	oak	1/2	(13)	1/2	(13)	108	(2743)	cut to length on 45°
24	2	crown moulding	oak	1/2	(13)	1 5/8	(41)	108	(2743)	purchase at local home-improvement store; cut to length on 45°
25	1	dresser top back rail	poplar	3/4	(19)	2 1/2	(64)	48 1/4	(1225)	
26	2	dresser top stiles	oak	3/4	(19)	3 1/4	(82)	22 1/2	(572)	
27	1	dresser top front rail	oak	3/4	(19)	6	(152)	48 1/4	(1225)	
28	6	drawer bottoms	melamine	3/4	(19)	20 1/4	(514)	22	(559)	
29	12	drawer sides	melamine	1/2	(13)	5 7/8	(149)	20 1/4	(514)	
30	12	drawer fronts and backs	melamine	1/2	(13)	5 1/8	(130)	22	(559)	
31	6	drawer faces	oak	3/4	(19)	6 1/2	(165)	24	(610)	
32	2	linen front stiles	oak	3/4	(19)	1 1/2	(38)	23 3/4	(603)	
33	1	linen front top rail	oak	3/4	(19)	2 3/4	(70)	18	(457)	
34	1	linen front bottom rail	oak	3/4	(19)	2	(51)	18	(457)	
35	1	linen right side	oak plywood	3/4	(19)	17	(432)	23 3/4	(603)	
36	1	linen bottom	oak plywood	3/4	(19)	17	(432)	19 1/4	(489)	
37	1	linen left-side back panel	oak plywood	1/4	(6)	17 1/4	(438)	23 3/4	(603)	
38	1	linen side front stile	oak	3/4	(19)	1 1/4	(32)	23 3/4	(603)	
39	1	linen side back stile	oak	3/4	(19)	2	(51)	23 3/4	(603)	
40	1	linen side top rail	oak	3/4	(19)	2 3/4	(70)	14	(356)	
41	1	linen side bottom rail	oak	3/4	(19)	2	(51)	14	(356)	
42	1	linen side middle stile	oak	3/4	(19)	2	(51)	19	(483)	
43	2	linen side inset panels	oak	3/4	(19)	6	(152)	19	(483)	
44	2	linen bottom support cleats	poplar	3/4	(19)	1 1/4	(32)	17	(432)	
45	1	linen back	oak plywood	1/4	(6)	20 1/2	(521)	23 3/4	(603)	
46	2	linen top cleats	poplar	3/4	(19)	2	(51)	19 1/4	(489)	
47	1	linen/TV top center	oak plywood	3/4	(19)	17 1/2	(445)	46 1/2	(1181)	
48	2	linen/TV top stiles	oak	3/4	(19)	3 1/4	(82)	21 1/2	(546)	

inches (millimeters)

REFERENCE	QUANTITY	PART	STOCK	THICKNESS	(mm)	WIDTH	(mm)	LENGTH	(mm)	COMMENTS
49	1	linen/TV top rail	oak	3/4	(19)	4	(102)	46 1/2	(1181)	
50	1	linen adjustable shelf	oak plywood	3/4	(19)	16 7/8	(429)	19 1/8	(486)	
51	2	linen door stiles	oak	3/4	(19)	2	(51)	19 1/2	(496)	
52	2	linen door rails	oak	3/4	(19)	2	(51)	14 1/2	(369)	
53	1	linen door center stile	oak	3/4	(19)	2	(51)	15 1/2	(394)	
54	2	linen door inset panels	oak	3/4	(19)	6 1/4	(159)	15 1/2	(394)	
55	1	linen door back	oak plywood	1/4	(6)	18 1/2	(470)	19 1/2	(496)	
56	2	TV front stiles	oak	3/4	(19)	1 1/2	(38)	23 3/4	(603)	
57	1	TV front top rail	oak	3/4	(19)	2 3/4	(70)	26	(660)	
58	1	TV front bottom rail	oak	3/4	(19)	2	(51)	26	(660)	
59	1	TV right-side back panel	oak plywood	1/4	(6)	19	(483)	23 3/4	(603)	
60	1	TV left side	oak plywood	3/4	(19)	19	(483)	23 3/4	(603)	
61	2	TV top & bott./door tracks	oak plywood	3/4	(19)	19	(483)	27 1/4	(692)	
62	1	TV back	oak plywood	1/4	(6)	23 3/4	(603)	28 1/2	(724)	
63	2	TV bottom cleats	poplar	3/4	(19)	1 1/4	(32)	19	(483)	
64	2	tambour door fillers	oak	3/4	(19)	1 3/4	(45)	21	(533)	
65	1	TV side front stile	oak	3/4	(19)	1 1/4	(32)	23 3/4	(603)	
66	1	TV side back stile	oak	3/4	(19)	2	(51)	23 3/4	(603)	
67	1	TV side top rail	oak	3/4	(19)	2 3/4	(70)	16	(406)	
68	1	TV side bottom rail	oak	3/4	(19)	2	(51)	16	(406)	
69	1	TV side middle stile	oak	3/4	(19)	2	(51)	19	(483)	
70	2	TV side inset panels	oak	3/4	(19)	7	(178)	19	(483)	
71	2	tambour door starter strips	oak	1/2	(13)	1	(25)	24	(610)	cut to length after gluing on the canvas
72	32	tambour door strips	oak	1/4	(6)	3/4	(19)	24	(610)	cut to length after gluing on the canvas

hardware

50' (16m)	5/8"-wide (16mm-wide) edge banding to match color of melamine
1	30" x 36" (762mm × 914mm) tambour door canvas
4	1/4" (6mm) shelf support clips
2	3/8" (10mm) backset hinges
3	doorknobs
6	drawer pulls
	glue
	6d finishing nails
	1 1/2" (38mm) screws
	finish nails
	clear finish

1 On the table saw, cut a ¼" notch into the inside back of the the two outside end panels so they can accept the ¼" back panel.

2 Assemble the face frame of the base cabinet. Then lay the face frame onto the ¼" dresser back panel and trace the face frame onto the back panel. This will give you reference lines for installing the drawer guides.

3 Glue and nail the face frame to the side panels. Install the back cleats with glue and nails. Then attach the ¼" back panel with the nails. Next, install the top cleats.

4 Lay out the pattern on the front base and cut it out. Then install the side and front bases. Cut the front and side base ledges to fit. Glue and attach with nails.

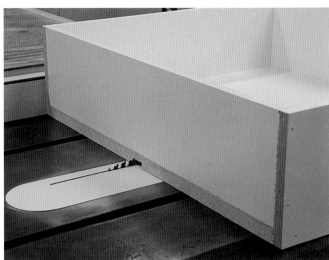

5 Cut the front and side base quarter-round moulding to fit. Glue and nail.

6 Assemble the drawers with glue and nails. Then cut the drawer guide groove in the center of all six drawer bottoms.

7 Install the drawer guides using an assembled drawer to center the drawer guides. Align the guides horizontally with the lines on the ¼" back panel.

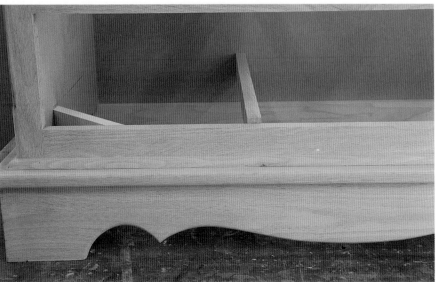

8 Using glue and nails, install two 8"-long 45° braces in the front lower left and right corners of the base cabinet, as shown.

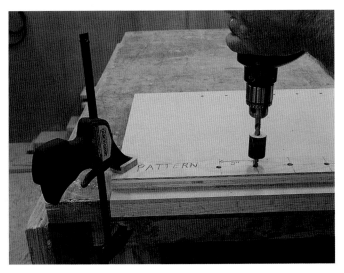

9 Make a drilling jig from a scrap piece of wood with ¼" holes 2" apart for the adjustable shelf brackets. Using this jig, drill ⅜"-deep holes (for the adjustable shelf support clips) in both sides of the linen cabinet section.

10 Assemble the linen cabinet face frame and the linen cabinet, then attach the face frame and install the back.

11 With your drill and a 2" hole saw, cut a hole in the lower center back of the linen cabinet back (for the electronic component's wires).

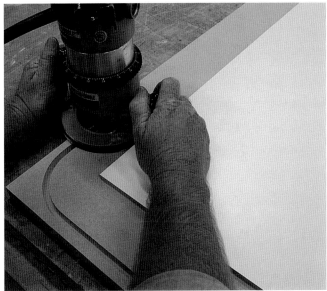

12 To cut the track for the tambour doors, use a scrap piece of plywood for a template. The track is cut ⅜" deep and ⅜" in from the sides and front edges of the TV's top and bottom panels. Install a ⅜" straight-cutting router bit in your router and measure the distance from the edge of your router base to the edge of the bit. Add ¾" to this distance and cut the plywood template to fit this distance in from both of the side edges and the front edge of the TV cabinet's top and bottom panels. Clamp the template to the panel and use it as your guide for the router. Carefully guide the router around the corner of the template to create the curves in the track. The track is a flattened U shape (see the technical illustration).

13 Rout a ¼" roundover on the outside front edges of the TV cabinet and the left edge of the linen cabinet. (Use a pipe clamp for a router stop.) Be sure the router bit does not hit the pipe clamp.

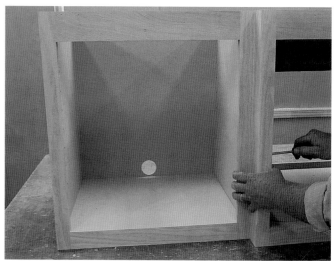

14 Screw the linen and TV cabinets together with 1½" screws.

15 Build the dresser top assembly. Round over the top and bottom of both side edges and the front edge using a ¼" roundover bit. Then, attach the assembly to the bottom of the linen/TV cabinet with 1½" screws.

16 Build the cabinet top assembly, then place the cabinet top (#47 in the materials list) onto the assembled linen/TV cabinet. Center the top side to side and locate the back edge of the top flush to the back of the cabinet assembly. Trace the offset of the linen/TV cabinet onto the bottom of the cabinet top. (Leave the same overhang all around the sides and front of the top.) Cut out the offset with your jigsaw. Sand this cut smooth and round over the top and bottom of the sides and front edges using a ¼" roundover bit in your router. Using 1¼" screws, attach the top to the linen and TV cabinet assembly.

17 Set your table saw blade to 45°. Set your miter gauge to 90° to cut the crown moulding. When you cut crown moulding on your table saw, pretend that the saw top is the cabinet face and the miter gauge is the cabinet top, then position the crown moulding to fit that visualized cabinet. Make some test cuts and check the fit.

18 Attach the crown moulding with glue and finish nails.

19 Cut the two tambour starter strips and all 32 tambour door strips. Round over the two front edges of all 32 strips with a $\frac{1}{8}$" roundover bit. Leave the two back edges square. If you don't have a router table, mount your router to a $\frac{1}{2}$" piece of particleboard with four legs to support the table. This works well as a temporary router table.

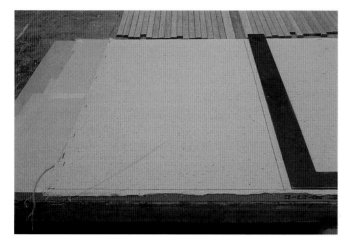

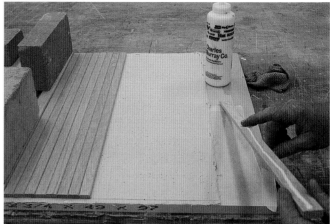

20 Cut a 32" × 38" piece of ½" particleboard. Cover the top of it with wax paper to keep the canvas from sticking to the particleboard when you glue on the tambour strips. Stretch the canvas tightly on the board and tack down the edges. Draw a line on the canvas ¾" in from the edge, parallel with the longer edge of the canvas. Use a square with one edge aligned with the line you just drew, and draw two lines ½" apart to separate the canvas into two equal sides, leaving a ½" space in the center.

21 Begin at the line in the center of the canvas and glue on the tambour door starter strip. Then glue on 16 tambour door strips as shown. Be careful to glue the pieces on the canvas only and not to each other! Repeat this process for the other door, leaving the ½" space in the center. Use weights to hold down the strips while the glue dries.

22 Use a razor blade to separate the two tambour doors along the ½" center strip of canvas. To cut one end of the doors square, place the starter strip against the stop of the sliding jig and hold a scrap piece of wood down on top of the tambour door to keep it from vibrating as you trim one edge. Repeat this for the other door. The sliding jig is a piece of plywood with a cleat at the back edge. The jig runs against the table saw fence.

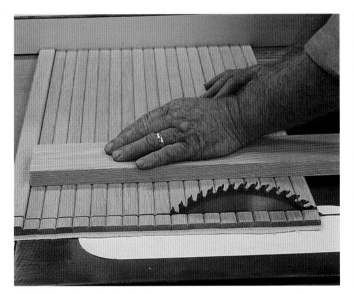

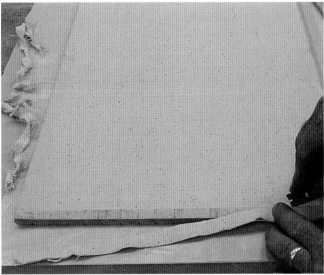

23 Measure the height inside the TV cabinet and add ⁵⁄₈" to this measurement. Cut the tambour doors to this height. Hold down the door with a scrap piece of wood as you cut.

24 Trim off ½" of canvas from the top and bottom of each door with a razor blade. Trim off any excess fibers from the back of the starter strip.

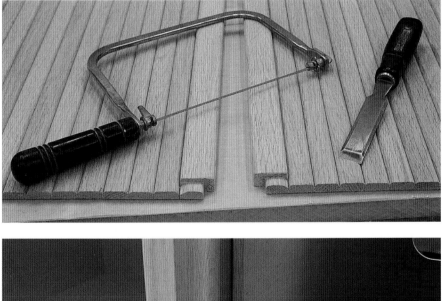

25 Use a coping saw and a chisel to trim ⁷⁄₁₆" off each end of the starter strips. Cut the end of the starter strip to ¼" × ¾".

{ *tip* } **Use dry graphite powder for lubricant in the tambour door tracks.**

26 Slide the tambour doors into the track from the back of the cabinet. Test fit the tambour door fillers. (The tambour door starter strips should just clear the fillers.) Then, attach the tambour door fillers to the back of the face frame to trim the tambour door opening. Disassemble and sand all the parts. Apply a clear finish. Put the top cabinet onto the dresser. Attach the drawer fronts with 1" screws from the inside of the drawer boxes. Hang the linen cabinet door, install the tambour doors and attach the back to the TV cabinet with screws. Install the drawer pulls and doorknobs and you're finished.

chippendale entertainment center

{ BY GLEN HUEY }

This entertainment center is the perfect example of a custom furniture concept. While I was building another piece similar to this one, I was approached by a woman who commissioned me to build this particular piece. She had an idea of the design she wanted, but had not been able to find an antique that exactly matched her imagination.

After evaluating a number of different cupboards, we began to incorporate aspects of each piece and apply them to one final piece, designed specifically for her.

The inclusion of the ogee feet, and especially the fluted corner columns, helps to propel this entertainment center straight to the top of its class.

FROM THE COLLECTION OF EILEEN ROBERTS, MANASSAS, VIRGINIA

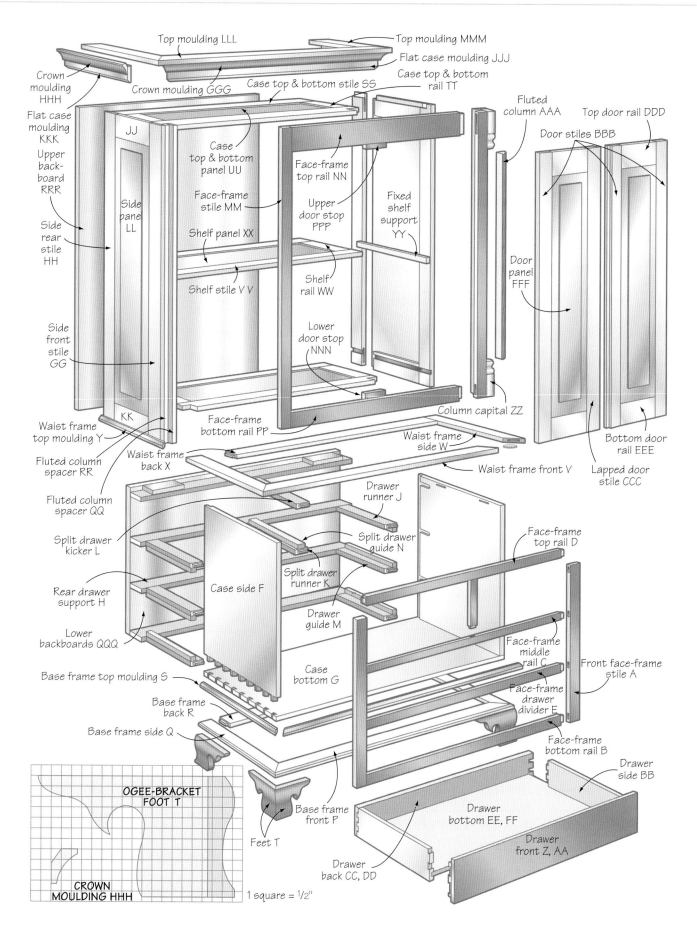

Top moulding LLL

Top moulding MMM

Flat case moulding JJJ

Crown moulding HHH

Crown moulding GGG

Case top & bottom stile SS

Case top & bottom rail TT

Fluted column AAA

Top door rail DDD

Flat case moulding KKK

JJ

Door stiles BBB

Upper backboard RRR

Case top & bottom panel UU

Face-frame top rail NN

Side panel LL

Side rear stile HH

Face-frame stile MM

Upper door stop PPP

Fixed shelf support YY

Door panel FFF

Shelf panel XX

Shelf stile V V

Shelf rail WW

Side front stile GG

Lower door stop NNN

Column capital ZZ

Bottom door rail EEE

KK

Waist frame top moulding Y

Face-frame bottom rail PP

Waist frame side W

Lapped door stile CCC

Fluted column spacer RR

Waist frame back X

Waist frame front V

Fluted column spacer QQ

Drawer runner J

Split drawer kicker L

Split drawer guide N

Face-frame top rail D

Rear drawer support H

Split drawer runner K

Case side F

Drawer guide M

Lower backboards QQQ

Base frame top moulding S

Case bottom G

Face-frame middle rail C

Front face-frame stile A

Base frame back R

Base frame side Q

Face-frame drawer divider E

Face-frame bottom rail B

Drawer side BB

OGEE-BRACKET FOOT T

Base frame front P

Feet T

Drawer bottom EE, FF

CROWN MOULDING HHH

1 square = 1/2"

Drawer back CC, DD

Drawer front Z, AA

inches (millimeters)

REFERENCE	QUANTITY	PART	STOCK	THICKNESS	(mm)	WIDTH	(mm)	LENGTH	(mm)	COMMENTS
LOWER SECTION										
A	2	front face-frame stiles	figured maple	$3/4$	(19)	2	(51)	$23^7/8$	(606)	
B	1	face-frame bottom rail	figured maple	$3/4$	(19)	$1^1/2$	(38)	$38^1/2$	(978)	1" (25mm) TBE
C	1	face-frame middle rail	figured maple	$3/4$	(19)	1	(25)	$38^1/2$	(978)	1" (25mm) TBE
D	1	face-frame top rail	figured maple	$3/4$	(19)	$1^1/4$	(32)	$38^1/2$	(978)	1" (25mm) TBE
E	1	face-frame drawer divider	figured maple	$3/4$	(19)	$1^1/4$	(32)	$8^3/8$	(213)	1" (25mm) TBE
F	2	case sides	figured maple	$3/4$	(19)	25	(635)	$23^7/8$	(606)	
G	1	case bottom	poplar	$5/8$	(16)	25	(635)	$40^1/2$	(1029)	
H	3	rear drawer supports	poplar	$3/4$	(19)	$2^1/4$	(57)	$39^9/16$	(1005)	
J	6	drawer runners	poplar	$3/4$	(19)	$2^1/4$	(57)	$23^1/4$	(590)	$3/8$" (10mm) TOE, 1" (25mm) TOE
K	1	split drawer runner	poplar	$3/4$	(19)	$3^1/4$	(82)	$23^1/4$	(590)	$3/8$" (10mm) TOE, 1" (25mm) TOE
L	1	split drawer kicker	poplar	$3/4$	(19)	$3^1/4$	(82)	$23^1/4$	(590)	$3/8$" (10mm) TOE, 1" (25mm) TOE
M	6	drawer guides	poplar	$5/8$	(16)	$1^1/8$	(28)	19	(483)	
N	1	split drawer guide	poplar	$5/8$	(16)	$1^1/4$	(32)	19	(483)	
P	1	base frame front	figured maple	$3/4$	(19)	3	(76)	$42^3/4$	(1086)	45° BE
Q	2	base frame sides	figured maple	$3/4$	(19)	3	(76)	$26^7/8$	(682)	45° OE
R	1	base frame back	poplar	$3/4$	(19)	3	(76)	$38^3/4$	(984)	1" (25mm) TBE
S	1	base frame top moulding	figured maple	$5/8$	(16)	$3/4$	(19)	56	(1422)	cut to fit
T	2	blanks for feet	figured maple	$1^3/8$	(35)	$5^3/4$	(146)	28	(711)	each blank makes three feet
U	2	rear foot braces	poplar	$3/4$	(19)	$5^3/4$	(146)	7	(178)	
V	1	waist frame front	figured maple	$3/4$	(19)	3	(76)	43	(1092)	45° BE
W	2	waist frame sides	figured maple	$3/4$	(19)	3	(76)	27	(686)	45° OE
X	1	waist frame back	poplar	$3/4$	(19)	3	(76)	39	(991)	1" (25mm) TBE
Y	1	waist frame top moulding	figured maple	$5/8$	(16)	$3/4$	(19)	56	(1422)	cut to fit
Z	2	drawer fronts	figured maple	$13/16$	(21)	$6^9/16$	(166)	$18^1/4$	(463)	$5/16$" (8mm) rabbet, three sides
AA	2	drawer fronts	figured maple	$13/16$	(21)	$6^9/16$	(166)	$37^1/8$	(943)	$5/16$" (8mm) rabbet, three sides
BB	8	drawer sides	poplar	$9/16$	(14)	$6^1/4$	(158)	20	(508)	
CC	2	top drawer backs	poplar	$9/16$	(14)	$5^1/2$	(140)	$17^1/2$	(445)	
DD	2	drawer backs	poplar	$9/16$	(14)	$5^1/2$	(140)	$36^7/16$	(925)	
EE	2	top drawer bottoms	poplar	$5/8$	(16)	$20^1/2$	(521)	$16^7/8$	(428)	
FF	2	drawer bottoms	poplar	$5/8$	(16)	$20^1/2$	(521)	$35^7/8$	(911)	
UPPER SECTION										
GG	2	side front stiles	figured maple	$3/4$	(19)	$2^3/4$	(70)	49	(1245)	
HH	2	side rear stiles	figured maple	$3/4$	(19)	$3^1/4$	(82)	49	(1245)	
JJ	2	side top rails	figured maple	$3/4$	(19)	$5^3/4$	(146)	20	(508)	$1^3/8$" (35mm) TBE
KK	2	side bottom rails	figured maple	$3/4$	(19)	$4^1/4$	(108)	20	(508)	$1^3/8$" (35mm) TBE
LL	2	side panels	figured maple	$5/8$	(16)	$17^7/8$	(454)	$39^5/8$	(1007)	
MM	2	face-frame stiles	figured maple	$3/4$	(19)	$2^3/4$	(70)	49	(1245)	
NN	1	face-frame top rail	figured maple	$3/4$	(19)	$5^3/4$	(146)	$32^3/4$	(832)	$1^3/8$" (35mm) TBE
PP	1	face-frame bottom rail	figured maple	$3/4$	(19)	$1^1/2$	(38)	$32^3/4$	(832)	$1^3/8$" (35mm) TBE
QQ	2	fluted column spacers	poplar	$3/4$	(19)	$1^1/2$	(38)	49	(1245)	
RR	2	fluted column spacers	poplar	$3/4$	(19)	$3/4$	(19)	49	(1245)	
SS	4	case top & bottom stiles	poplar	$3/4$	(19)	$3^1/2$	(89)	$37^7/16$	(951)	
TT	4	case top & bottom rails	poplar	$3/4$	(19)	3	(76)	$18^{15}/16$	(481)	$1^1/4$" (32mm) TBE
UU	2	case top & bottom panels	poplar	$3/4$	(19)	$17^1/8$	(435)	$32^1/8$	(816)	$3/8$" (10mm) TAS
VV	6	shelf stiles	poplar	$3/4$	(19)	3	(76)	$36^3/4$	(933)	
WW	6	shelf rails	poplar	$3/4$	(19)	3	(76)	18	(457)	$1^1/4$" (32mm) TBE

inches (millimeters)

REFERENCE	QUANTITY	PART	STOCK	THICKNESS	(mm)	WIDTH	(mm)	LENGTH	(mm)	COMMENTS
UPPER SECTION, CONT'D										
XX	3	shelf panels	poplar	$3/4$	(19)	$16^1/8$	(409)	$31^3/8$	(797)	$3/8$" (10mm) TAS
YY	2	fixed shelf supports	poplar	$3/4$	(19)	2	(51)	$21^5/8$	(549)	
ZZ	4	column capitals	figured maple	$1^1/2$	(38)	$1^1/2$	(38)	9	(229)	glue four pieces together, then turn and separate
AAA	4	fluted columns	figured maple	$1^1/4$	(32)	$1^1/4$	(32)	36	(914)	glue four pieces together, then turn and separate; need only two pieces
BBB	3	door stiles	figured maple	$3/4$	(19)	$2^3/4$	(70)	$41^3/4$	(1060)	
CCC	1	lapped door stile	figured maple	$3/4$	(19)	$3^1/8$	(79)	$41^3/4$	(1060)	
DDD	2	top door rails	figured maple	$3/4$	(19)	$2^3/4$	(70)	$12^1/4$	(311)	$1^3/8$" (35) TBE
EEE	2	bottom door rails	figured maple	$3/4$	(19)	$3^1/2$	(89)	$12^1/4$	(311)	$1^3/8$" (35) TBE
FFF	2	door panels	figured maple	$5/8$	(16)	$10^1/8$	(257)	$36^1/8$	(917)	
GGG	1	crown moulding	figured maple	$3/4$	(19)	$2^1/2$	(64)	45	(1143)	cut to fit
HHH	2	crown moulding	figured maple	$3/4$	(19)	$2^1/2$	(64)	29	(737)	cut to fit
JJJ	1	flat case moulding	figured maple	$7/16$	(11)	$2^1/8$	(54)	40	(1016)	cut to fit
KKK	2	flat case moulding	figured maple	$7/16$	(11)	$2^1/8$	(54)	26	(660)	cut to fit
LLL	1	top moulding	figured maple	$3/4$	(19)	$3^1/4$	(82)	45	(1143)	cut to fit
MMM	2	top moulding	figured maple	$3/4$	(19)	$3^1/4$	(82)	29	(737)	cut to fit
NNN	1	lower door stop	figured maple	$3/4$	(19)	$3/4$	(19)	4	(102)	
PPP	1	upper door stop	figured maple	$1/2$	(13)	4	(102)	4	(102)	
QQQ	1	lower backboard	poplar	$5/8$	(16)	$23^1/4$	(590)	$39^7/8$	(1013)	assembled pieces
RRR	1	upper backboard	poplar	$5/8$	(16)	48	(1219)	$37^3/4$	(959)	assembled pieces

TBE = Tenon Both Ends

TOE = Tenon One End

TAS = Tenon All Sides

BE = Both Ends

OE = One End

hardware

6	antique finish rosette pulls	item #H-10FB	Horton Brasses
2	antique finish stirrup pulls	item #H-40	Horton Brasses
2 pairs	3" (76mm) antique finish H-hinges	item #HH-2	Horton Brasses
8	$1/4$" (6mm) shelf supports (standard)		
	No. 8 × $1^1/4$" (32mm) slot-head wood screws		
	glue		
	#20 biscuits		
	5d finishing nails		
	wood clips		
	ball catch		
	water-based aniline dye		
	lacquer sanding sealer		
	lacquer top coat		

1 Cut the top, middle and bottom rails and the face-frame sides for the lower section according to the plan, then create the mortise-and-tenon joints to connect all the pieces.

2 Test fit the face-frame pieces and mark all areas where mortises need to be cut to accept the drawer runners and kickers.

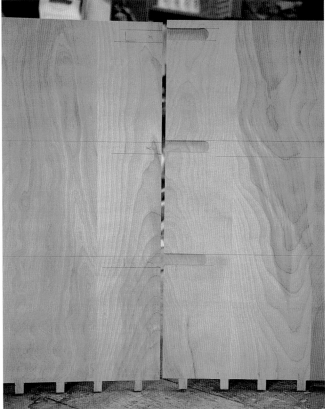

3 With those mortises created, it is time to assemble the lower-section face frame. Make sure to square the unit by checking for equal measurements on the diagonal. After the glue sets, drill 1/4"-diameter holes in the frame at the tenons. Then, using 1/4"-square maple pegs partially sharpened in a pencil sharpener, peg the joints in the face frame.

4 Take the sides of the lower section and cut on each bottom edge the pins that will match with the dovetails on the case bottom. Locate the rear drawer dividers and top drawer kicker rails on each side. Be sure to create a pair of matching sides and rout a short 3/4" by 1/4"-deep groove to accept the rails, then cut the 3/4" by 1/4"-deep rabbet for the backboards.

5 Mill the case bottom and cut the corresponding dovetails. Then assemble and glue the sides to the bottom.

6 When the side/bottom unit is dry, it is time to attach the face-frame assembly on the front edge. Pay attention to lining up the routed rear divider slots with the face frame to ensure level running drawers.

7 Mill the drawer runner pieces to size, including the tenon work, and create a pocket screw hole to attach the runner to the side of the case. Here, I built a simple jig that lays the piece at a 15° angle. Using a ³⁄₄" Forstner bit, start the hole, stopping at the appropriate level to use a No. 8 × 1¼" slot-head wood screw. Finish predrilling the hole with a smaller bit.

8 Glue the front tenon into place, and slide the rear drawer divider into the slot and over the runner's rear tenon. Then nail through the rear divider and into the case side at a slight angle.

9 Install the screw through the pocket hole and into the case side for additional support. With all the pieces in place, size, cut and install the drawer guides so they are flush with the face-frame sides. Don't forget the center guide for the split top drawers. Then sand the unit to 180 grit.

10 Mill and assemble the foot base frame by creating mortise-and-tenon joints at the back corners and biscuited 45° cuts at the front corners.

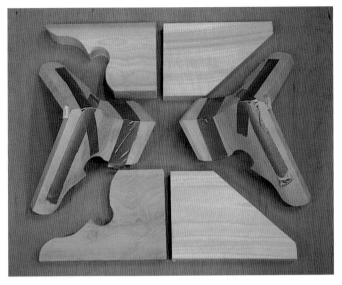

11 Make the ogee-bracket feet. (See the sidebar "Ogee-Bracket Feet" later in this chapter.)

12 Sand the foot base frame, then fit the ogee-bracket feet to the frame with glue and corner blocks. Rout the profile on the edge of the frame.

13 After the foot base has been completed, invert the lower case unit and attach the foot assembly to the case bottom with No. 8 x 1¼" screws in the front frame. Use nails to complete the assembly. Nails allow slight movement over time, which helps keep the piece from splitting. Notice the corner blocks on the feet.

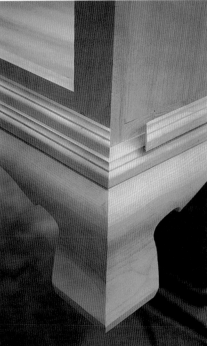

14 Next, mill and install the base moulding that covers the exposed case dovetails.

15 Make the lower-section top frame just as you did the foot base frame, and cut the profile with a combination of a thumbnail bit and a ³⁄₁₆" roundover bit.

16 Nail sized filler pieces to the bottom of the top frame at the back rail, then finish-sand the top frame and attach it to the lower section with wood clips and screws into the filler pieces.

17 Now build the drawers for the lower section of the entertainment center.

18 Turning to the upper section, mill the frame pieces of the sides to width; but before you cut to length, create the roundover detail on the interior edge of the pieces. Next, lay out and cut the ¼"-wide mortises in all stiles.

19 Set the blade to 45°. Cut just to the shoulder of the roundover cut on all rails (a single pass creates the tenon area) and stiles (nibble away for the mortises). Reset the blade to 90° and complete the tenons.

20 Adjust the fence to remove the roundover edge, and cut just up to the angle created in the piece.

21 Set the saw blade depth to ³⁄₈" and run a ¹⁄₄"-wide groove in all pieces to capture the raised panels. Check the fit and check the measurements for the panels.

22 Mill and cut the raised panels, and when the edges have been finish-sanded to 180 grit, glue and assemble the side units.

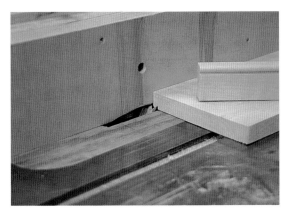

23 Make the upper-section front face frame just as you did the side unit frames, but without the groove for the panels. Also, use a bead detail on the interior edge instead of a roundover. This allows the doors to be framed within a beaded border.

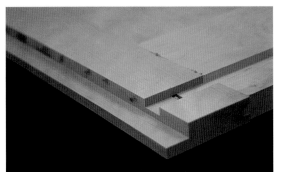

24 When the sides are dry, locate where the top and bottom panels fit, and cut a ³⁄₄" x ¹⁄₄" dado for each. Then cut the ⁷⁄₁₆" x ³⁄₄" rabbet for the backboards.

25 Make the L-shaped corner that will create the area for the fluted columns, and attach it to the front inside edge of the side units.

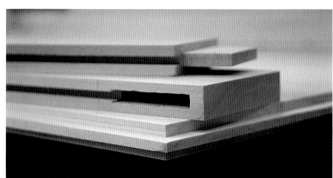

27 Mill, cut to size and assemble the top and bottom panels as well as the two shelves. All are made in the same fashion, with the front and back pieces being the stiles and the ends being the rails.

26 When set, glue the front face frame to the other leg of the L-corner, creating the quartered column area.

28 Notch the top and bottom around the L-corner to fit tightly against the face frame.

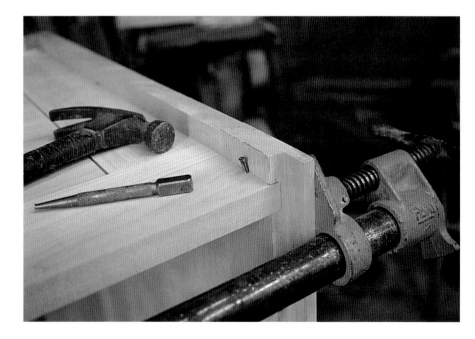

29 Sand, then slide the top panel into the side unit dadoes. Nail through the panels into the case sides at a slight angle.

30 Locate and install a fixed shelf support on each side of the upper case to hold the shelf in place. Use screws to attach the shelf to the cleats.

31 Using a piece of pegboard, drill the holes for the adjustable shelf supports that are used with the adjustable shelf. Be sure to orient the template properly. I start with the template at the top and skip down approximately 8" to the first hole, then drill every other hole. I figure a 12" adjustment area.

32 To make the turn-fluted quartered columns, start by gluing together four pieces of wood equal in size, in this case $1\frac{1}{2}$" square by 9" in length. The trick is to place a piece of brown paper bag between the 4 pieces. After the glue has dried, turn to profile.

33 After turning the column capitals, simply separate the pieces with a chisel and a firm tap from a mallet. For the capitals, you need to use all four resulting pieces: two at the top and two at the bottom.

34 Assemble and turn the pieces for the fluted portion of the columns. Place duct tape around each square end for support, then turn a place in the center to size and add tape there, as well. Continue turning until the column is rounded to size, removing the tape as necessary.

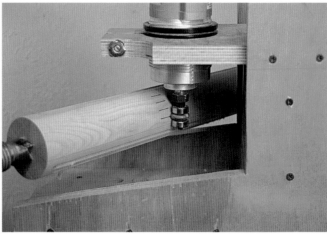

35 To flute two portions of the column, use a fluting bit in a trim router mounted in a wooden cradle layout. You will use only two pieces. When you're done, separate the finished pieces.

36 Install the upper capitals with glue and clamps as shown in the plan. Then cut the fluted portion of the column to size, and glue and nail the piece into place.

37 Finish the columns by cutting the base capital to size and gluing it into place.

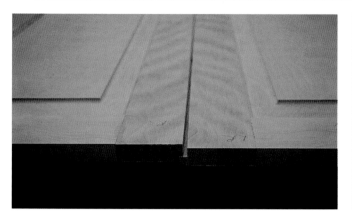

38 Make the doors. Once fit to the face frame, the half-lap detail is added to the center stile on each door.

39 Create the top moulding of the cupboard using a ¹/₂" roundover bit. The moulding is attached to the case by first cutting the 45° angles on each end of the front piece and on one end of the side pieces, then biscuit cuts are made in each angle cut. Next attach the front piece with glue and screws (No. 8 x 1¹/₄" wood screws), then fit the side pieces, glue at the biscuit areas, and screw the ends to the case.

40 Invert the case on the top and apply the first stage moulding to the case with nails. Next, make and cut the crown moulding and nail to both the case and the top moulding.

41 Place the upper section on top of the lower section. Align the upper section into place, making it flush in the back and equally spaced on each side. Mill and cut to fit the waist moulding that is attached to the lower section with nails and that allows the upper section to slide into the three-sided space. Remember to allow a sanding disc's width between the upper case and the moulding on each side, so you can easily maneuver the large upper case. Also install the doorstop pieces shown in the center of the opening. They are at the top and bottom of the door area.

lacquer finishing

>> To finish a piece in lacquer, first finish-sand the piece to 180 grit, then wet the entire piece in order to raise the grain. When dry, lightly sand a second time with the 180 grit. Next, select a water-based aniline dye stain that is mixed according to directions and thoroughly soak the piece of furniture. Allow to sit until almost dry, then remove any excess stain. Once the stain has dried, lightly sand with a 400-grit paper to knock down the fuzzies.

Now spray a heavy coat of lacquer sanding sealer. When the sealer is dry, sand the entire piece with a 320-grit paper or a 400-grit sponge. Remove all the dust with a tack cloth.

Thin the lacquer top coat to the desired consistency and spray several coats (usually four or five), being sure to allow drying time between each coat. If necessary, sand problem areas prior to the final coat. A single-edge razor blade helps eliminate runs or sags.

I like to use a "dull-rubbed-effect" lacquer for my pieces. I believe it best simulates an antique-style finish. I also spray with a high-volume, low-pressure (HVLP) unit.

42 Now make the backboards for the cupboard. Remember that the upper-section back pieces are shorter than the lower section's. All pieces are half-lapped. After all the pieces are sanded, then apply the finish (see "Lacquer Finishing" above).

{*tip*} Locate the holes for your particular hardware and counterbore a ⅝" hole in the backside of the drawer front with a Forstner bit. This allows the hardware to be flush on the interior of the drawer; so no snagging of your clothes!

43 After you have applied the finish to the entertainment center, you need to install the appropriate hardware. Here you see the H-hinges. Lay the hinge so that one leg of the hinge is on the door stile, with the other on the face frame. Predrill for the screws and install. Also install the rosette pulls on the drawers, the stirrup pulls on the doors and the ball catch on the doorstop at the top of the door opening.

making ogee-bracket feet

STEP 1   Draw the ogee foot design on the end of your stock and set the blade height. Set the temporary fence so that the blade enters and exits the stock in line with the design, and make multiple passes over the blade, removing the waste.

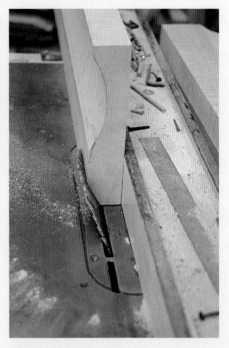

STEP 2   Use the saw to trim as close to the design as possible, then remove any additional waste with a plane or scraper. Rough sand to a finished profile.

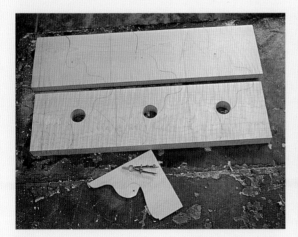

STEP 3   Using a pattern, lay out the feet, making sure that you have the pieces for three pairs. Drill the appropriate hole size, and cut the foot profile.

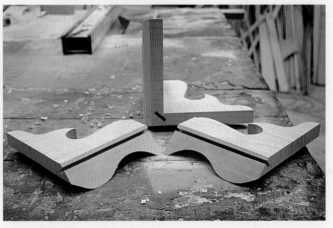

STEP 4   Cut for a spline in each pair of feet as shown, and assemble.

entertainment center

{ BY DANNY PROULX }

Analyze these modules, break down the larger sections into small components, and I believe you will see that this project isn't as complicated as it looks.

This entertainment center was built to suit my needs. There are large cubes for speakers, a wide tower for a 32" television, a pullout for a record turntable, and many CD and tape storage drawers. Your needs may be different, so alter the partitions accordingly.

The pullout has full-extension drawer glides. The large television is mounted on a lazy-Susan-style mechanism that's available in most hardware stores. The component areas are fitted with smoked glass doors to allow most remote controls to operate with the doors closed.

I decided to use ³⁄₄" oak plywood veneer board. It's strong and can withstand greater loads than particleboard over wide shelf spans. Plywood-core veneer board is more expensive than particle core, but I believe it's warranted in this case.

I also considered how to hide the large television and decided pocket doors were the best option. I'll detail how these sliders are mounted.

I purchased factory-made wood doors and had 5mm gray glass with polished edges fabricated for my glass doors.

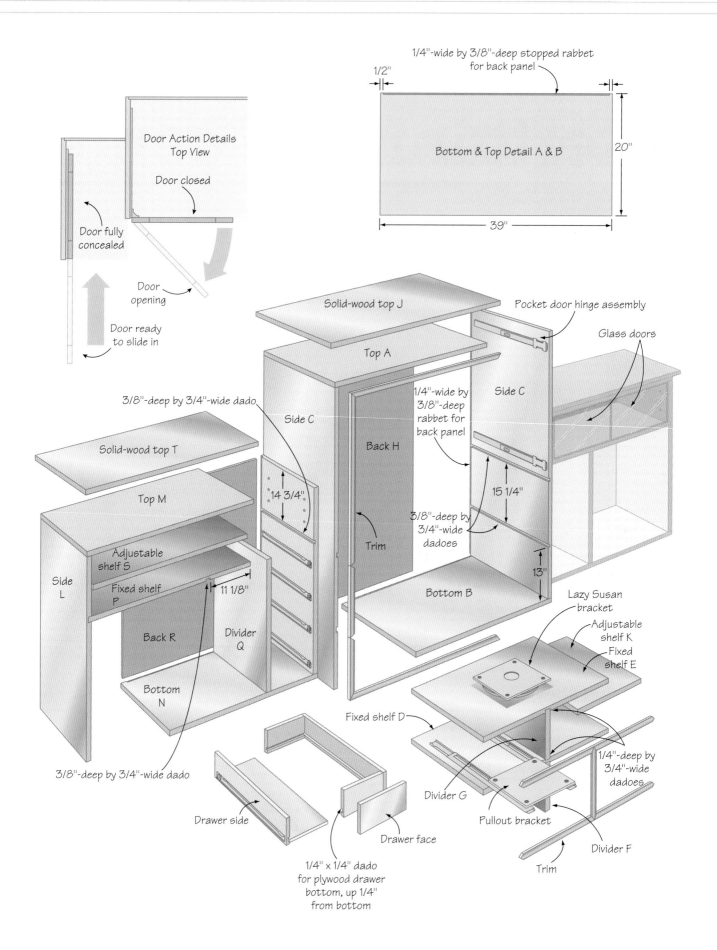

Door Action Details
Top View

Door closed

Door fully
concealed

Door
opening

Door ready
to slide in

1/4"-wide by 3/8"-deep stopped rabbet
for back panel

1/2"

Bottom & Top Detail A & B

20"

39"

Solid-wood top J

Pocket door hinge assembly

Top A

Glass doors

3/8"-deep by 3/4"-wide dado

Side C

1/4"-wide by
3/8"-deep
rabbet for
back panel

Side C

Solid-wood top T

Side C

Back H

Top M

14 3/4"

15 1/4"

Adjustable
shelf S

Side
L

Fixed shelf
P

Trim

3/8"-deep by
3/4"-wide
dadoes

13"

11 1/8"

Back R

Divider
Q

Bottom B

Lazy Susan
bracket

Bottom
N

Adjustable
shelf K

Fixed
shelf E

3/8"-deep by 3/4"-wide dado

Fixed shelf D

1/4"-deep by
3/4"-wide
dadoes

Drawer side

Divider G

Divider F

Pullout bracket

Trim

Drawer face

1/4" x 1/4" dado
for plywood drawer
bottom, up 1/4"
from bottom

Building the Center Tower

inches (millimeters)

REFERENCE	QUANTITY	PART	STOCK	THICKNESS	(mm)	WIDTH	(mm)	LENGTH	(mm)	COMMENTS
A	1	top	veneered ply	$^3/_4$	(19)	28	(711)	38	(965)	
B	1	bottom	veneered ply	$^3/_4$	(19)	28	(711)	38	(965)	
C	2	sides	veneered ply	$^3/_4$	(19)	28	(711)	$65^1/_2$	(1664)	
D	1	fixed shelf	veneered ply	$^3/_4$	(19)	$27^3/_4$	(705)	$37^1/_4$	(946)	
E	1	fixed shelf	veneered ply	$^3/_4$	(19)	$27^3/_4$	(705)	$37^1/_4$	(946)	
F	1	divider	veneered ply	$^3/_4$	(19)	$13^1/_4$	(336)	$27^3/_4$	(705)	
G	1	divider	veneered ply	$^3/_4$	(19)	$15^3/_4$	(400)	$27^3/_4$	(705)	
H	1	back	veneered ply	$^1/_4$	(6)	$37^1/_8$	(943)	$66^1/_8$	(1679)	
J	1	solid-wood top	oak	$^3/_4$	(19)	29	(737)	40	(1016)	
K	1	adjustable shelf	veneered ply	$^3/_4$	(19)	$18^1/_8$	(460)	27	(686)	
	1	base	veneered ply	$^3/_4$	(19)	26	(660)	34	(864)	
	1	TV turntable platform	veneered ply	$^3/_4$	(19)	$18^1/_2$	(470)	$28^1/_2$	(724)	
	1	pullout platform	veneered ply	$^3/_4$	(19)	$16^7/_8$	(428)	18	(457)	

hardware

1	1" × 12" (25mm × 305mm) oak side trim
2	1" × 12" (25mm × 305mm) oak side trim
26' (8mm)	$^3/_4$"-wide (19mm-wide) trim
2	$18^1/_4$" × $35^1/_2$" (463mm × 902mm) TV pocket doors
2	$17^3/_4$" × 13" (451mm × 330mm) album storage doors
2	$14^{13}/_{16}$ × $17^3/_4$ (377mm × 451mm) glass doors
	1" and 2" (25mm and 51mm) wood screws
	brad nails
	carpenter's glue
	preglued iron-on edge tape
	decorative bolts
	plastic wire grommets
	$^3/_8$" (10mm) wood plugs
2 sets	20" (508mm) pocket door hardware
	hidden hinges
6	doorknobs
1 set	lazy-Susan hardware
2 sets	pullout hardware
4	door catches
	$1^1/_4$" (32mm) wood screws
	glass-door hinges and handles

1 Cut the top A and bottom B. Each board will require a ¼"-wide by ⅜"-deep stopped dado to receive the back panel. Stop the dado ½" from each end. The top of the bottom board B and the bottom of the top board A must each be dadoed. Then apply preglued iron-on edge tape to both ends of boards A and B.

2 Cut the two tower sides C. Both sides require dadoes and a back rabbet on each inside face. All the cuts are ⅜" deep. Refer to the diagram for rabbet and dado positions.

3 Prepare fixed shelf D by cutting dadoes ¼"-deep by ¾"-wide, centered on both the top and bottom. Handle this board carefully, as it will be weak at the cut until it's installed. Shelf E is cut like shelf D; however, only one dado is needed in the center on the bottom face. Then attach the top A and bottom B to the tower sides C, making certain all dadoes and rabbets are properly aligned. Use glue and 2" wood screws. Predrill the screw holes.

4 Install shelves D and E in their respective dadoes. Use carpenter's glue and screw through the outside of the cabinet sides into the shelves using 2" wood screws. Start your screws 10" back from the front edges so the screws will be hidden by the side towers.

6 Next, install the ¼" back H in the rabbets. Apply a fine bead of glue and secure the board with brad nails. This board must be cut square, as it will help to correctly align the cabinet.

5 Cut and install dividers F and G. Apply glue and clamp in place until they set.

7 We need a strong base to support the large television, equipment and record albums that will be stored in the unit. I want to slightly elevate the unit but still maintain as much contact with the floor as possible. To achieve this, install a ¾" base to the underside of bottom B. Attach the base 2" in from the sides and front with glue and 1¼" wood screws.

8 Trim the outside front and side edges of the base with ¾"-thick by 1"-wide solid wood. Attach these strips to the cabinet base with glue and 1¼" wood screws. The side pieces need to be only 12" long because the side towers cover a portion of the center tower.

Building the Side Towers

Two side towers are required. They are mirror images of each other in my project. If you plan to build the same setup, mark the right and left pieces to avoid mistakes.

inches (millimeters)

REFERENCE	QUANTITY	PART	STOCK	THICKNESS	(mm)	WIDTH	(mm)	LENGTH	(mm)	COMMENTS
L	4	sides	veneered ply	3/4	(19)	20	(508)	44 1/2	(1131)	
M	2	tops	veneered ply	3/4	(19)	20	(508)	39	(991)	
N	2	bottoms	veneered ply	3/4	(19)	20	(508)	39	(991)	
P	2	fixed shelves	veneered ply	3/4	(19)	19 3/4	(502)	38 1/4	(971)	
Q	2	dividers	veneered ply	3/4	(19)	19 3/4	(502)	29 3/8	(747)	
R	2	backs	veneered ply	1/4	(6)	38 3/4	(984)	45 1/8	(1146)	
S	2	adjustable shelves	veneered ply	3/4	(19)	19	(483)	37 3/8	(950)	
T	2	solid-wood tops	oak	3/4	(19)	21	(533)	40	(1016)	
	2	bases	veneered ply	3/4	(19)	18	(457)	38	(965)	

hardware

2	1" × 39" (25mm × 991mm) front trim
2	1" × 18" (25mm × 457mm) side trim
56' (18m)	3/4"-wide (19mm-wide) trim
2	10 5/8" × 28 7/8" (270mm × 733mm) wood doors
4	14 15/16" × 18 5/8" (380 × 473mm) glass doors
	2" (51mm) wood screws
2	doorknobs
4	hidden hinges
	shelf pins
	brad nails
	1" (25mm) wood screws

1 Cut the four sides L and rout the dadoes and rabbets on the inside face of each panel. You will need two right and two left side panels. The tops M and bottoms N are the same size. Cut the 1/4"-wide by 3/8"-deep stopped dado on the underside of the top boards M and top side of the bottom boards N as shown. Mark the panels, noting their final position, and apply oak tape to the edge that will be visible.

2 Cut the two fixed shelves P and rout the dado as shown in the technical drawing. Secure the tops M and bottoms N to the side panels. Use glue and 2" wood screws in piloted holes from the top and bottom of each board. Verify that the finished edges are oriented properly on each tower.

3 Install the middle fixed shelves P in the dadoes. Remember, there is a right and left position for each shelf in the towers. Apply glue to the joint and clamp until dry. The shelves are set flush with the front edges of the side panels.

{ *tip* } Cut a board ¹/₁₆" higher than the upper cavity dimension and carefully wedge it in place over the vertical divider dado joint. The pressure will tighten the joint until it sets.

4 Cut the vertical divider panels Q and glue them into the dado. The bottom ends of each panel are glued and 2" wood screws are installed from the underside of the bottom board to secure the dividers. Make certain the divider is parallel to the side panel. The panel must be accurately positioned to permit proper fitting of the inset doors. Next, install the ¼" back panel R using glue and brad nails. Attach the ¾" plywood base to the side towers in the same way the center tower base was installed. However, it's positioned 2" in from the one side and front edges of the cabinets. The base should extend 1" past the side that attaches to the center tower. The extended base will meet the center tower base. (Remember to install right and left bases.) Then install the base trim as shown here.

Connecting the Towers

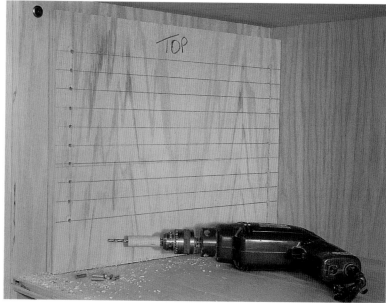

2 Build a shelf pin-hole jig from scrap lumber. I've used 1" on-center spacing. A short length of dowel rod on my drill bit guarantees the correct hole depth.

1 Secure the sides L to the center tower using decorative bolts. Many styles are available, so choose one that matches the cabinet hardware.

3 Plastic wire grommets are available at most hardware stores. Install them in shelves and partitions so all the equipment can be connected.

Building and Installing the Solid-Wood Tops

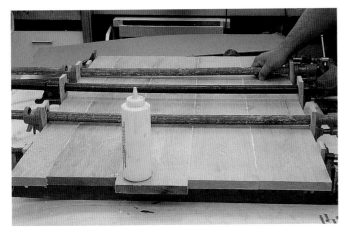

1 The solid-wood tops J and T can be purchased in standard sizes at many home-improvement stores. If you have the clamps available, tops can be made by edge-gluing a number of boards together. If you don't have the equipment to dress the edges, many lumberyards will provide that service for a small fee.

2 Cut the tops J and T to size according to the materials lists and sand all the surfaces smooth. Then install each top with six 1" wood screws in predrilled holes from inside the cabinet. Counterbore the holes before installing the screws so they can be filled with wood plugs.

Installing the Edge Trim

The trim I've used is available in most lumber stores. It's ³⁄₄" wide, with a moulded pattern on the face.

1 Attach the trim with glue and an electric brad nailer if you have one. If not, use ³⁄₄" brads and set the nails. Use a 45° miter at all right-angled corners.

2 When a shelf intersects a vertical panel, a special cut is required. The moulding meeting a run at 90° is cut at a 45° angle when it's in the standing position on your miter box. The back cut allows the intersecting run to fit tightly. The cut may require a little sanding, and the angle is dependent on the style of moulding used. It's a little fussy at times and requires a few trial cuts to get a good fit.

Installing the Glass Doors

Before ordering or making doors, build
the cabinet. Inset doors must be correctly sized for a proper fit. The door
spacing depends a great deal on the
type of hinge hardware. To get a perfect fit, purchase the hardware and
make a sample door with scrap lumber.

1 Install the glass-door hinges. I've used an inset-style hinge that
doesn't require holes drilled in the glass.

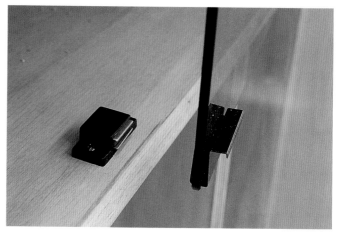

2 The door handles I've used slip onto the glass and are held in
place with a foam gasket.

Fitting the Wood Inset Doors

1 The hardware I've used for this project is a traditional North
American–style inset hinge.

2 Install the hinges 2" from the bottom and top edges of the door. Shim the door in its proper open position and secure the door to the cabinet. Most hinges will provide a little adjustment, so install screws in the center of the adjustment slot. Test the door operation and adjust if necessary. Install the remaining doors using the same procedure.

Attaching the Pocket Doors

I've used pocket door hardware by Blum for this project. Follow the manufacturer's installation procedures that are included with your hardware.

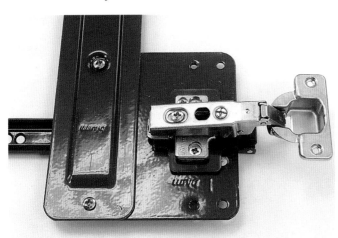

1 Assemble the right and left door hardware sets according to the instructions.

3 Attach the door and test for proper operation. The hidden hinges allow the doors to be adjusted in three directions. Quite often, adjustment and trial fitting is necessary when installing pocket doors.

2 My doors are ³/₄" thick, so I have set the door stops 1" back from the front edge of the cabinet. That distance includes ³/₄" for the door thickness and ¹/₄" for the hinge hardware. Attach the top rail with one screw in the front hole. Measure the same setback for the bottom rail bumper and install a screw in the front of that rail. Level the top rail and secure the back with a screw. Before securing the bottom rail, check the roller operation, making sure the mechanism hits the bottom and top bumper at the same time. If it's operating correctly, install the track screws.

{ *tip* } You can accurately locate the hinge positions on the door by first attaching the hinge body to the door hardware. Next, locate and mark the center of the hinge with a marker pen on the hinge flange. Hold or shim the door in its correct open position and transfer that mark to the door. Both hinges should be marked on the door. The Blum hinges supplied with the pocket door set recommend that the 35mm hole in the door be set back ³/₁₆" from the edge of the door. Drill the holes and install both hinges.

Attaching a Television Lazy Susan

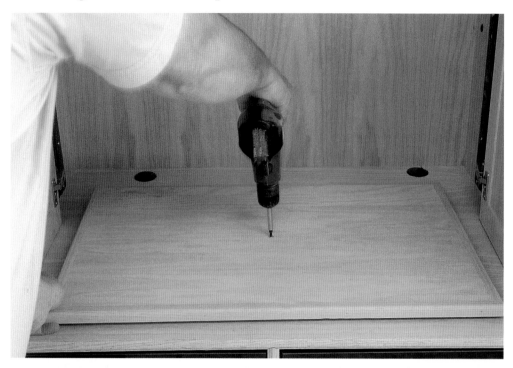

1 The size and style of a lazy-Susan platform depends on the hardware you purchase. Each manufacturer has a different method, so read the installation instructions with your hardware.

2 My television platform for the lazy-Susan hardware is a ¾"-thick piece of veneer plywood. You can apply edge tape or attach ½"-thick solid-wood strips to all four edges, as I've done.

{*tip*} If you use the solid-wood edging for your television platform, round over the top edges. The wood strips can be attached with glue and finishing nails. Set the nails and fill the holes with a colored putty stick that matches your final finish.

Making a Turntable Pullout

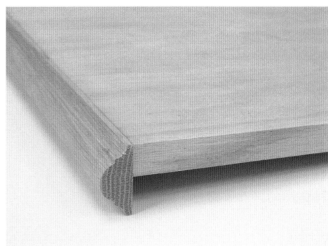

1 Whenever you install pullouts behind cabinet doors, attach a ³⁄₄" wood spacer. That spacer allows the pullout enough clearance to move past the door hinges. This spacer or cleat is required only on the hinge side. Remember to reduce the cabinet width by ³⁄₄" when calculating the pullout width.

2 Build the pullout platform using ³⁄₄"-thick veneer plywood with taped edges. The front on my platform has decorative moulding applied, which can be used as a handle.

3 Install two strips of ³⁄₄" x 1¹⁄₂" wood on the bottom of the pullout. The spacing depends on which style of drawer glides you are using. Mine require ¹⁄₂" on each side. Therefore, the support distance equals the cabinet interior width, minus the wood spacer and the ¹⁄₂" clearance per side for the drawer glides.

4 I've installed full-extension, side-mounted drawer glides. Be sure to set the pullout back far enough into the cabinet so the inset glass door can close properly.

factors determining drawer width

> > Most drawer glides require ½" clearance on both sides to operate. That means the drawer box exterior dimensions must be 1" less than the opening. Because we have to use wood cleats for the door clearance, we must also subtract the width of the cleat when calculating drawer sizes. My drawer box width equals a side-to-side cabinet measurement of 10½", minus the thickness of the ¾" cleat, less the ½" per side spacing for drawer hardware. In this example, the drawer box is 9" wide.

Building Storage Drawers

Drawers are a great addition to any entertainment center. They help organize all the CDs, audiocassettes, videocassettes and associated hardware.

These drawers are simple boxes made of cabinet-grade ½"-thick plywood. I have attached a drawer face to the box that matches the cabinet material.

inches (millimeters)

REFERENCE	QUANTITY	PART	STOCK	THICKNESS	(mm)	WIDTH	(mm)	LENGTH	(mm)	COMMENTS
	8	cleats	hardwood	¾	(19)	1½	(38)	18¾	(476)	
	16	sides	Baltic birch	½	(13)	3	(76)	18	(457)	
	8	fronts	Baltic birch	½	(13)	3	(76)	8	(203)	
	8	backs	Baltic birch	½	(13)	2½	(64)	8	(203)	
	8	bottoms	Baltic birch	¼	(6)	8½	(216)	17¾	(451)	
	8	drawer faces	veneered ply	¾	(19)	9⅞	(251)	3½	(89)	

hardware

8 sets	18" (457mm) full-extension side-mounted drawer guides
	1" and 1½" (25mm and 38mm) wood screws
	finishing nails
	carpenter's glue

1 Attach the eight cleats to the cabinet on the door-hinge side. Use three 1½" wood screws per cleat and space them 6" apart, starting from the bottom board. Then cut all the sides, fronts and backs from ½" Baltic birch plywood, as detailed in the materials list. Make a ¼"-wide by ¼"-deep groove ¼" above the bottom edge of each side and front board.

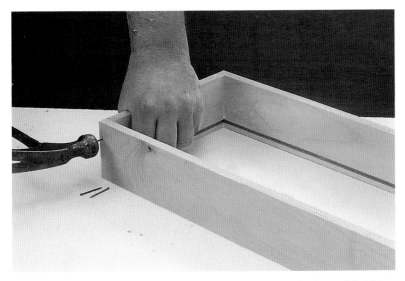

2 For each drawer, attach the side boards to the front with glue and finishing nails. Check that the grooves for the bottom are aligned before nailing.

3 Install the back with glue and nails. It is ½" lower and its top edge is aligned with the side board's top edges.

4 Slide the bottom into the grooves. It should be flush with the back face of the back when correctly positioned. Use finishing nails to secure it to the back panel.

5 Cut and install the drawer front. Use 1" screws from the inside to secure the front to the box.

Completing the Cabinet

Remove all the hardware, fill any nail holes, and give the cabinet a final sanding before finishing. To finish the piece, I used a 50-percent mixture of Minwax Provincial #211 and Puritan Pine #218 stains. After staining, I applied three coats of polyurethane.

After the finish is dry, install the hardware. Drawer glides should be installed according to the manufacturer's instructions. All the pullout hardware in my unit is 18" full-extension side-mounted glides. They provide full access to the drawers where my CDs and cassettes will be stored.

remodeled

playroom

{ BY RICK WILLIAMS }

When we moved into our home, we used one of the bedrooms as a playroom for our two small children. But a funny thing is happening; those two small children aren't so small anymore.

One day my son and I were on our way to a Boy Scout meeting and were talking about the playroom. We decided that it would make a great room for an entertainment center and home office.

After a lot of sweet-talking my wife and a promise that it would take only about a month to remodel, we started on our room. As I mentioned, we also decided to incorporate our computer and home office into our room, but feel free to design whatever works for you. I've found that getting a cup of coffee and sitting in the room to be remodeled early in the morning (when all is still quiet) works well, and will help you visualize your options. With a little planning, your design will be perfect for your family's needs.

We used a Philips 31" HDTV, Sony VCR player and Sony five-disc CD changer with Dolby Surround Sound for our entertainment center. These units work great, but to be honest we picked them because they were on sale. The best thing about remodeling a room to meet your changing needs is that you can incorporate whatever fits into your budget at the time. If you know you can't afford a big-screen TV, but plan on buying one in the future, you can leave enough room for updates.

I recommend that you go to an electronics superstore during your planning stage to look at everything that is available, then decide what you like and can afford to add to your room. Once you have purchased your equipment, then you can position it and build around it.

If you spend your money wisely, you can expect to spend around four thousand to six thousand dollars on your remodeled room, but rest assured, your family will get all the money back in enjoyment, not to mention the increase in value to your home.

After we decided what we wanted our new room to look like, I
built this unit with tons of bookshelf space and enough room for
the TV that we picked out.

We also picked out a fireplace
my wife had been wanting for
some time. This was a particu-
larly nice addition. It keeps the
room plenty warm in the winter and adds a nice decorative
touch.

We decided to put a home office into our remodeled room. With plenty of forethought you can add everything your family needs, including tons of extra space for surfing the Internet and paying bills.

tv cabinet

with lift

{ BY JIM STACK }

This entertainment center has a feature that sets it apart from all the others in this book — the remote-control lift for the television.

The lift makes it easy to hide the television when it's not in use, and when the television is needed, no doors need to be opened. The lift also raises the viewing level of the television.

I finished this entertainment center with a black gloss lacquer to enhance the slick effect of the lift as the television rises. Using a solid color enhances the effect of the mouldings that dress up this unit. Shadow lines break up the cabinet into interesting patterns. This effect would not be as pronounced if the unit had a stained finish. However, if a nice stained hardwood entertainment center unit is what you had in mind, this design would be perfect!

All the materials used to make this entertainment center are available at any home-improvement center. Make yourself a shopping list, gather the materials, back your vehicle to the door, load it up and you're good to go.

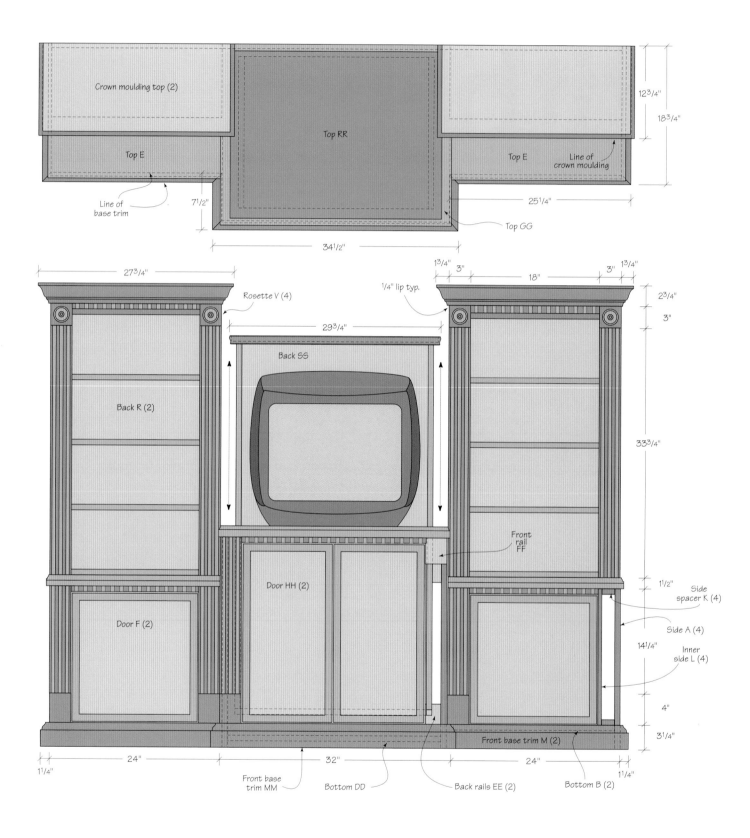

Crown moulding top (2)

Top RR

Top E

Top E

Line of crown moulding

12³/₄"

18³/₄"

Line of base trim

7¹/₂"

25¹/₄"

Top GG

34¹/₂"

27³/₄"

Rosette V (4)

1³/₄" 3"

18

3" 1³/₄"

2³/₄"

3"

1/4" lip typ.

29³/₄"

Back SS

Back R (2)

33³/₄"

Front rail FF

1¹/₂"

Side spacer K (4)

Door HH (2)

Side A (4)

Door F (2)

Inner side L (4)

14¹/₄"

4"

Front base trim M (2)

3¹/₄"

24"

32"

24"

1¹/₄"

1¹/₄"

Front base trim MM

Bottom DD

Back rails EE (2)

Bottom B (2)

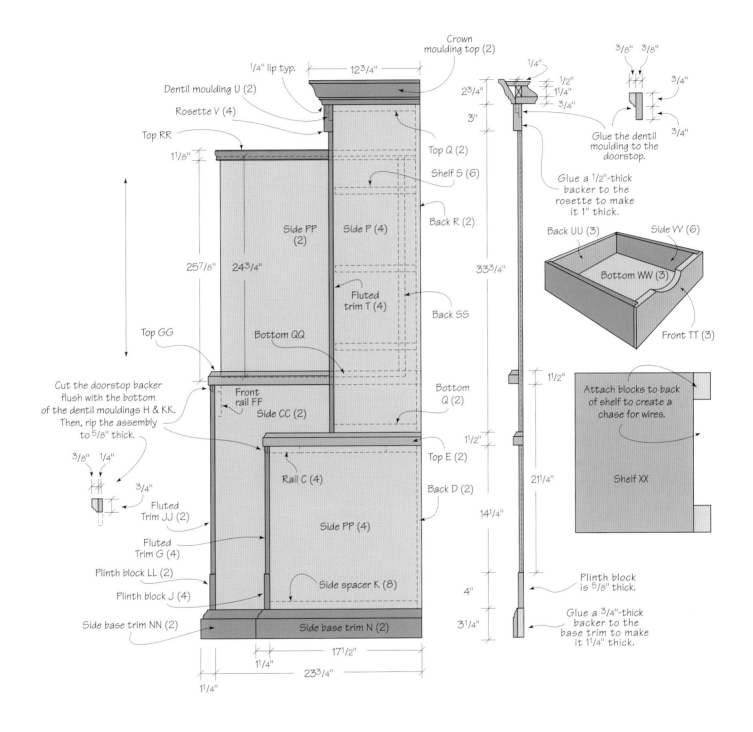

Crown moulding top (2)

1/4" lip typ.

12³/4"

Dentil moulding U (2)

Rosette V (4)

Top RR

1¹/8"

Top Q (2)

Shelf S (6)

Side PP (2)

Side P (4)

Back R (2)

25⁷/8"

24³/4"

33³/4"

Fluted trim T (4)

Back SS

Top GG

Bottom QQ

Cut the doorstop backer flush with the bottom of the dentil mouldings H & KK. Then, rip the assembly to ⁵/8" thick.

Front rail FF

Side CC (2)

Bottom Q (2)

1¹/2"

3/8"   1/4"

3/4"

Rail C (4)

Top E (2)

Fluted Trim JJ (2)

1¹/2"

Fluted Trim G (4)

Back D (2)

21¹/4"

Plinth block LL (2)

Side PP (4)

Plinth block J (4)

Side spacer K (8)

14¹/4"

Side base trim NN (2)

Side base trim N (2)

4"

17¹/2"

3¹/4"

1¹/4"

23³/4"

1¹/4"

Crown moulding top (2)

1/4"

2³/4"

1/2"
1¹/4"
3/4"

3"

3/8" 3/8"

3/4"

3/4"

Glue the dentil moulding to the doorstop.

Glue a ¹/2"-thick backer to the rosette to make it 1" thick.

Back UU (3)

Side VV (6)

Bottom WW (3)

Front TT (3)

Attach blocks to back of shelf to create a chase for wires.

Shelf XX

Plinth block is ⁵/8" thick.

Glue a ³/4"-thick backer to the base trim to make it 1¹/4" thick.

inches (millimeters)

REFERENCE	QUANTITY	PART	STOCK	THICKNESS	(mm)	WIDTH	(mm)	LENGTH	(mm)	COMMENTS
BASE CABINETS										
A	4	sides	plywood	$^3/_4$	(19)	$17^1/_2$	(446)	$21^3/_4$	(552)	
B	2	bottoms	plywood	$^3/_4$	(19)	17	(432)	$22^1/_2$	(572)	
C	4	rails	plywood	$^3/_4$	(19)	3	(76)	$22^1/_2$	(572)	
D	2	backs	plywood	$^1/_2$	(13)	$23^1/_2$	(597)	$18^1/_4$ h	(464)	
E	2	tops	plywood	$1^1/_2$	(38)	$24^1/_4$	(616)	$18^1/_4$ d	(465)	dim. include $^3/_4$"-thick (19mm-thick) buildup & $^3/_4$" × $1^1/_2$" (19mm × 38mm) edging
F	2	doors	plywood	$1^1/_4$	(32)	$17^{11}/_{16}$	(449)	$17^3/_4$	(450)	thickness dimension includes the applied mouldings
G	4	fluted trim	hardwood	$^1/_2$	(13)	3	(76)	$14^1/_2$	(368)	
H	2	dentil mouldings	hardwood	$^5/_8$	(16)	$^3/_4$	(19)	18	(457)	
J	4	plinth blocks	hardwood	$^5/_8$	(16)	3	(76)	4	(102)	
K	8	side spacers	plywood	$^3/_4$	(19)	$1^1/_2$	(38)	17	(432)	
L	4	inner sides	plywood	$^1/_2$	(13)	17	(432)	$18^1/_2$	(470)	
M	2	front base trim	hardwood	$1^1/_4$	(32)	$3^1/_4$	(83)	$25^1/_4$	(641)	thickness includes backer, outside & inside miter cuts, one each end
N	2	side base trim	hardwood	$1^1/_4$	(32)	$3^1/_4$	(83)	$18^3/_4$	(476)	thickness includes backer, outside miter cut, one end
BOOKCASES										
P	4	sides	plywood	$^3/_4$	(19)	10	(254)	$36^3/_4$	(933)	
Q	4	tops and bottoms	plywood	$^3/_4$	(19)	$9^1/_2$	(241)	$22^1/_2$	(572)	
R	2	backs	plywood	$^1/_2$	(13)	$23^1/_2$	(597)	$36^3/_4$ h	(933)	
S	6	shelves	plywood	$^3/_4$	(19)	$9^1/_4$	(235)	$22^7/_{16}$	(570)	
T	4	fluted trim	hardwood	$^1/_2$	(13)	3	(76)	$33^3/_4$	(857)	
U	2	dentil mouldings	hardwood	$^5/_8$	(16)	$^3/_4$	(19)	18	(457)	
V	4	rosettes	hardwood	1	(25)	3	(76)	3	(76)	thickness includes $^1/_2$"-thick (13mm-thick) backer
CROWN MOULDING TOPS										
W	2	bottom plates	plywood	$^3/_4$	(19)	$10^1/_2$	(267)	$23^3/_4$	(603)	
X	2	long crown mouldings	hardwood	$^9/_{16}$	(14)	$3^1/_4$	(83)	$27^1/_2$	(699)	miter both ends
Y	4	short crown mouldings	hardwood	$^9/_{16}$	(14)	$3^1/_4$	(83)	$12^1/_2$	(318)	miter one end, make two right & two left
Z	4	front & back frame strips	plywood	$^3/_4$	(19)	$1^1/_4$	(32)	$23^3/_4$	(603)	
AA	6	cross frame strips	plywood	$^3/_4$	(19)	$1^1/_4$	(32)	9	(229)	
BB	2	top plates	plywood	$^1/_2$	(13)	$11^{11}/_{16}$	(297)	$25^{15}/_{16}$	(659)	35° angle on one long and two short edges
TELEVISION CABINET										
CC	2	sides	plywood	$^3/_4$	(19)	$23^3/_4$	(603)	$28^1/_2$	(724)	
DD	1	bottom	plywood	$^3/_4$	(19)	$23^3/_4$	(603)	$30^1/_2$	(775)	
EE	2	back rails	plywood	$^3/_4$	(19)	6	(152)	$30^1/_2$	(775)	
FF	1	front rail	plywood	$^3/_4$	(19)	$^3/_4$	(19)	$30^1/_2$	(775)	
GG	1	top	plywood	$1^1/_2$	(38)	$24^1/_2$	(622)	$32^1/_2$	(826)	see illustration for details of top construction
HH	2	doors	plywood	$1^1/_4$	(32)	$12^7/_8$ +/-	(327)	$24^1/_2$	(622)	thickness dimension includes the applied mouldings
JJ	2	fluted trim	hardwood	$^1/_2$	(13)	3	(76)	$21^1/_4$	(540)	
KK	1	dentil moulding	hardwood	$^3/_4$	(19)	$1^1/_2$	(38)	26	(660)	
LL	2	plinth blocks	hardwood	$^5/_8$	(16)	3	(76)	4	(102)	
MM	1	front base trim	hardwood	$1^1/_4$	(32)	$3^1/_4$	(83)	$34^1/_2$	(876)	thickness includes backer, two outside miter cuts, one each end
NN	2	side base trim	hardwood	$1^1/_4$	(32)	$3^1/_4$	(83)	$7^1/_2$	(191)	thickness includes backer, outside & inside miter cuts, one each end
TELEVISION LIFT BOX										
PP	2	sides	plywood	$^3/_4$	(19)	$21^1/_4$ d	(540)	$24^3/_4$ h	(629)	$^1/_2$" × $^3/_4$" (13mm × 19mm) rabbet in back edge
QQ	1	bottom	plywood	$^3/_4$	(19)	$21^1/_4$ d	(540)	$27^3/_4$ w	(705)	
RR	1	top	plywood	$1^1/_8$	(29)	$22^5/_8$	(575)	$29^3/_4$	(756)	dimensions include mouldings applied to edges
SS	1	back	plywood	$^3/_4$	(19)	$24^3/_4$ h	(629)	$27^1/_4$ w	(692)	

hardware

4 sets	1¹⁄₂" × 2" (38mm × 51mm) butt hinges
3 sets	16" (405mm) full-extension drawer glides
32	5mm black shelf supports item #22955 Rockler
1	Television lift (size is builder's choice)
4	³⁄₈"-diameter (10mm-diameter) bullet catches
4	3" × 3" (76mm × 76mm) rosettes
12' (4m)	3¹⁄₄" (83mm) crown moulding
16' (5m)	3"-wide (76mm-wide) fluted door casing
9' (3m)	³⁄₈" × ³⁄₄" (10mm × 19mm) dentil moulding
9' (3m)	³⁄₈" × 1¹⁄₂" (10mm × 38mm) doorstop
12' (4m)	¹⁄₂" × 3¹⁄₄" (13mm × 83mm) base trim
8' (3m)	⁵⁄₁₆" × 1¹⁄₈" (8mm × 29mm) plywood edge moulding
	1¹⁄₂" (38mm) and 1¹⁄₄" (32mm) drywall screws
	glue
	staples
4	³⁄₈" × 1¹⁄₂" (10mm × 38mm) dowels
	spackling compound
	primer
	top coat

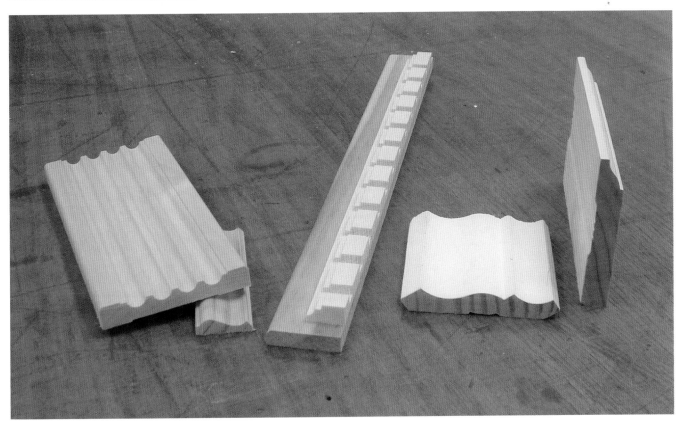

These mouldings are available at any home-improvement center. They are, left to right: 3"-wide fluted door casing, 1¹⁄₈"-wide plywood edge moulding with the lip trimmed off the back, 1¹⁄₂"-wide doorstop used to back the ³⁄₈" x ³⁄₈" dentil moulding, 3¹⁄₄" crown moulding and 3¹⁄₄" base trim.

1 Cut out the parts per the cutting list. Cut the rabbets in the back edges of the sides using the table saw. Measure ½" from the saw's fence to the outside of the blade and set the blade's height at ½". Make the first cut as shown.

2 Turn the part on its side and make the second cut. The rabbet will be exactly ½" by ½". Make test cuts in scrap wood to be sure your setup is correct.

3 Drill pocket holes in the top sides of the rails, in the top sides of the top panels and in the bottom sides of the bottom panels on the bookcases.

4 Use a 2½"-wide spacer to locate the bottom panels on the two outside base cabinets.

cabinet back panels

>> Cut the cabinet backs squarely. Then, when they are attached to the cabinets, they will automatically square the cabinet. When attaching the back panels to the cabinets, start at one corner of the cabinet. Hold the bottom edge of the back panel flush with the bottom of the cabinet and attach along this edge with screws. Then, adjust the side of the cabinet that is at a right angle to the bottom until it is flush with the side of the back. Install screws along this edge. The cabinet should now be square. Install screws along the opposite side and top of the cabinet.

5 Attach the bottoms of the base cabinets to the cabinet sides with screws. These holes will be covered by the base.

6 Attach the rails using screws (and glue if you want). These joints are strong with or without glue.

7 Attach the cabinet backs with screws.

8 Cut the base trim into rough finished lengths and glue them to ¾-thick plywood backer boards. The added thickness to the base provides a wider top edge for the plinth blocks.

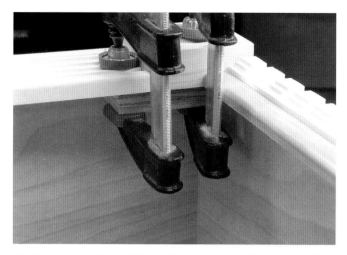

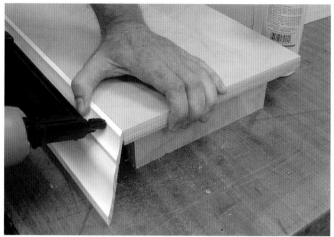

9 Glue the dentil moulding to the doorstop as shown in the illustration. Then attach the fluted trim, rosettes and dentil moulding assemblies to the front edges of the cabinets. Glue ¾" x 2" x 3" blocks at the joints of the fluted trim and rosette on the bookcases.

10 Cut out the parts for the crown moulding assemblies. See the sidebar "Cutting Miters on Crown Moulding." Attach the crown moulding to the bottom plate with glue and staples, nails or screws.

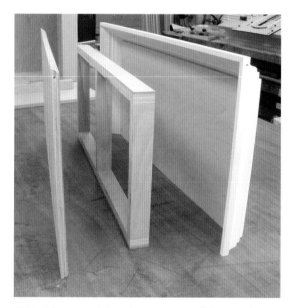

12 Glue the subassemblies together and place a heavy weight on the whole thing. This is a simple but effective clamping arrangement.

11 After attaching the crown moulding to the top plate, make two frames to fit inside the crown moulding on top of the top plate. The width of the strips for the frame should let the upper plate rest about ¼" below the top edge of the crown moulding when the assembly is put together. See the illustration for details.

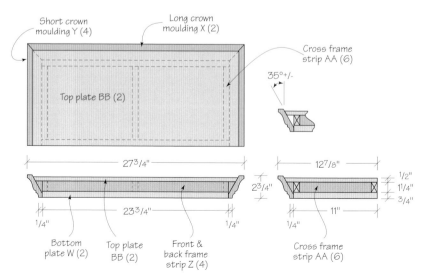

cutting miters on crown moulding

STEP 1 Place the moulding face-in against the fence and the bottom of the saw's bed, as shown in the photo. Then attach a ledger strip to the bed. This will hold the moulding at the proper angle and keep it from slipping.

STEP 2 Set the saw at a 45° angle to the bed and make a test cut.

STEP 3 Set the saw to the opposite 45° angle and make another test cut on a piece of moulding. This piece sits the same way against the ledger strip as the first piece of moulding.

STEP 4 Check the fit of the test cuts. Hold the part of the moulding that rested against the ledger strip flat against the edge of the plywood. (It's easier to make this crown assembly upside down on your bench.) If the miter is open at the top of the moulding (where the moulding is resting on the bench), move the ledger strip slightly away from the saw's fence. If the miter is open at the bottom of the moulding, move the ledger strip slightly closer to the saw's fence.

13 Glue the base trim on the front and side of the two small base cabinets. Be sure to make left and right cabinets. Glue the side spacers at the top and bottom of these base cabinets. Then nail the inner sides to the spacers.

14 Nail the plinth blocks and fluted trim to the base cabinet front edges. Then, glue the dentil moulding assembly to the front edge of the top rail. See the illustration for the dentil moulding details.

15 Cut buildup strips to fit the base cabinet tops and glue and staple (or screw) them to the underside of the tops. Plane or sand the edges of the buildup strips flush to the edges of the tops.

16 Cut the edge strips to fit the tops and glue them to the edges of the tops. See the illustration for top details.

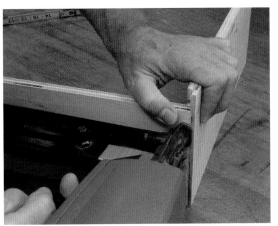

17 Install the drawer glides in either the right or left base cabinet. Use a spacer to help hold the hardware parallel to the bottom of the cabinet. Then cut another spacer that you can sit on top of the glide you just installed, and install the next drawer glide. Do the same for the top drawer glide. Repeat this process for the opposite side of the cabinet. See the illustration for details on the location of the drawer glides.

18 Cut the drawer parts to size. Cut a rabbet in the ends of the drawer front and the back ends of the sides. Attach the sides to the front using glue and staples. Then, attach the drawer back to the sides. Slide the bottom into place and check the drawer for squareness by measuring the drawer at the diagonals. Attach the bottom with staples at the bottom of the back. (Do not use glue to install the bottom.) Finally, attach the drawer glides to the sides of the drawer box, locating them about halfway up from the bottom of the drawer box. Install the drawers in either base cabinet (your choice) and install the shelves in the other base cabinet.

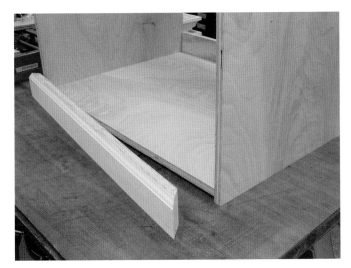

19 Following the instructions that came with the TV lift, assemble the lift. Double-check, and if necessary, triple-check the measurements of the lift. Then, cut the parts for the TV cabinet. To measure for the location of the bottom of the cabinet, raise the lift and measure the uppermost point of elevation. (Allow for the thickness of the bottom of the TV lift box bottom that will be sitting on the top of the lift.) Note in the photo that the bottom of the cabinet is only 1" above the floor. This space was needed inside the cabinet to accommodate the lift. Assemble the cabinet. Set the lift in the cabinet. Lower and raise the lift to be sure all is correct. Use two rails at the back of the cabinet instead of a solid back. (This will help at installation time when you need access to cable and electricity.) Cut and install the front base trim.

20 Note that the top front rail is 3½" wide and is mounted vertically. After the plinth blocks and fluted trim have been installed, cut the rail to ¾" wide using a jigsaw. Using a wider front rail makes it easier to assemble the cabinet because the rail can be attached with two screws at each side of the cabinet, and the fluted trim has more contact area on the rail. Also, note the hardwood buildup strip that will be glued to the inside back of the base trim, plinth blocks and fluted trim. This adds strength and thickness to the mouldings.

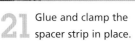
21 Glue and clamp the spacer strip in place.

22 Assemble the bookcases. Install the lift in the center cabinet. Attach the side base cabinets to the center cabinet with screws. Screw the tops and the bookcases to each of the side cabinets. Then, cut and glue the two base trim returns to the center cabinet.

23 Assemble the TV lift box, install it on the TV lift and raise the lift to its fully elevated position. Double-check all measurements for the top of the center cabinet. One of the side strips for the top has been placed on the top of the center cabinet to show the relationship of the edge trim to the TV lift box. The top of the bottom panel of the TV lift box will be flush with the top of the cabinet.

24 Disassemble the cabinets and set the center cabinet on its back. Then, glue the top to the cabinet. This makes it easier to locate the top and to use clamps to hold it in place while the glue dries.

25 Reattach the cabinets to one another. Glue the dentil moulding assembly to the ¾"-wide front rail on the center cabinet. Double-check the measurements for the doors. Cut out the doors, then cut the plywood edge moulding to fit the faces of the doors. (The plywood edge moulding used on the doors has a lip on it. It is called plywood edge moulding at the home-improvement center. This lip is cut off before it is used on this project. See illustration for a detailed drawing.) Glue and staple or nail it in place. Hold the moulding flush to the edges of the doors.

DETAIL OF TELEVISION CABINET TOP

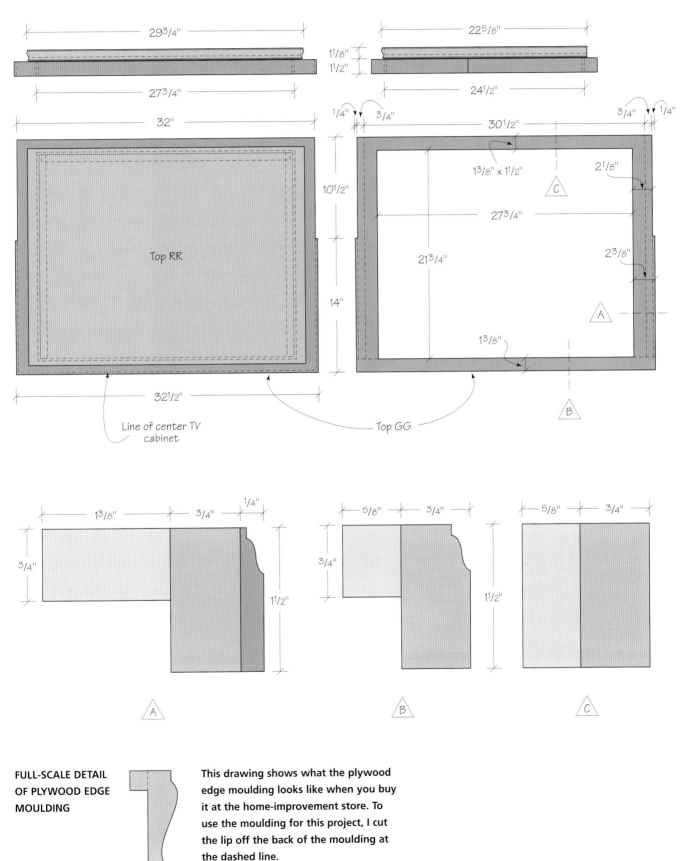

Line of center TV cabinet

Top RR

Top GG

13/8" × 11/2"

FULL-SCALE DETAIL OF PLYWOOD EDGE MOULDING

This drawing shows what the plywood edge moulding looks like when you buy it at the home-improvement store. To use the moulding for this project, I cut the lip off the back of the moulding at the dashed line.

26 Trim the moulding flush to the edges of the doors. Then, using the table saw or a router, cut a mortise in the side edges of the doors. The hinges are located at the top and bottom edges of the doors. I feel this makes the hinges less obtrusive. You could also use knife hinges if you choose.

27 When installing the butt hinges, open the hinge to 90° so the leaf rests against the face of the trim on the front of the door. This locates the hinge barrel far enough forward on the door so the door will swing open a full 180°.

28 Cut the top for the TV lift box. The finished top should be 2" longer and 2" wider than the opening for the box. Use the same trim you used on the doors to edge this top.

29 Use dowels to attach the top to the TV lift box. Install the dowels in the top edges of the box's sides. Drill slightly oversize holes in the top. Then set the top on the box, using the dowels to hold the top in place.

**DETAIL OF CABINET
DOOR HINGING**

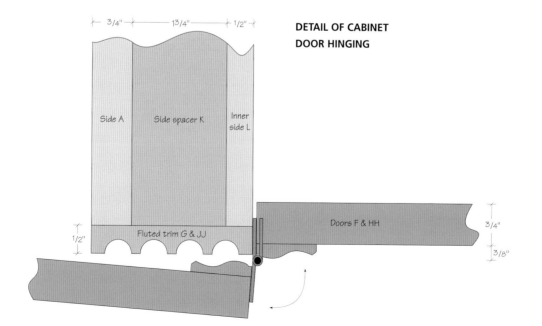

30 This is the TV lift box top in place. If you like, you can add buildup to the top, then attach the moulding. That would eliminate the gap between the top of the side and bottom of the top.

31 Fill all nail holes, cracks and dings with spackling compound. After the spackling has dried, sand it smooth.

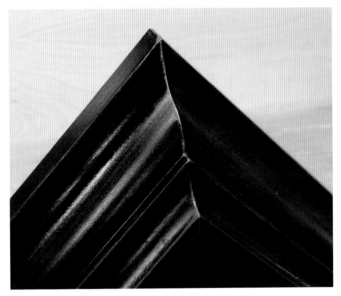

32 Apply a primer. The primer has lots of solids in it, so when it dries it can be sanded smooth with 320-grit sandpaper. Apply another coat of primer if needed and sand it smooth when dry. What you want to do is make the surfaces of your project as smooth as you can.

33 When the top coat is applied, it should lie smoothly on the prepared surface with little or no sanding needed. Apply two or three coats of top coat.

{*cabinet tip*} **The TV lift is a powerful mechanical device that can cause serious physical harm if operated when the cabinet doors are open. If small children are in the household, it is recommended that a fixed panel be installed on the front of the cabinet or that the doors have child-proof locks installed.**

SUPPLIERS

ADAMS & KENNEDY — THE WOOD SOURCE
6178 Mitch Owen Road
P.O. Box 700
Manotick, Ontario, Canada K4M 1A6
613-822-6800
www.wood-source.com
Wood supply

ADJUSTABLE CLAMP COMPANY
417 North Ashland Avenue
Chicago, Illinois 60622
312-666-0640
www.adjustableclamp.com
Clamps

BALL AND BALL
463 West Lincoln Highway
Exton, Pennsylvania 19341
800-257-3711
www.ballandball-us.com
Hardware reproductions

B&Q
B&Q Head Office
Portswood House
1 Hampshire Corporate Park
Chandlers Ford
Eastleigh
Hampshire
SO53 3YX
023 8025 6256
www.diy.com
Tools, paint, wood, electrical, garden

BEARING DISTRIBUTORS, INC.
8000 Hub Parkway
Cleveland, Ohio 44125
216-642-9100
www.bdi-usa.com
Bearings

BIESEMEYER WOODWORKING TOOLS
216 South Alma School Road, Suite 3
Mesa, Arizona 85210
800-782-1831
www.biesemeyer.com
Fences, guards, splitters

CONSTANTINES WOOD CENTER OF FLORIDA INC.
1040 East Oakland Park Boulevard
Fort Lauderdale, Florida 33334
800-443-9667
www.constantines.com
Tools, wood, veneers, hardware

DELTA MACHINERY
4825 Highway 45 North
P.O. Box 2468
Jackson, Tennessee 38302-2468
800-223-7278 (U.S.)
www.deltawoodworking.com
Woodworking tools

EXAKTOR PRECISION WOODWORKING TOOLS, INC.
136 Watline #1 & 2
Mississauga, Ontario, Canada L4C 2E2
800-387-9789
www.exaktortools.com
Accessories for the table saw

FORREST MANUFACTURING COMPANY, INC.
457 River Road
Clifton, New Jersey 07014
800-733-7111
forrest.woodmall.com
Carbide-tipped saw blades, dado sets, sharpening

FREUD TOOLS
218 Feld Avenue
High Point, North Carolina 27263
800-334-4107
www.freudtools.com
Carbide-tipped saw blades, dado sets, tooling

GARRETT WADE CO., INC.
161 Avenue of the Americas
New York, New York 10013
800-221-2942
www.garrettwade.com
General hand tools and supplies, some power tools

THE HOME DEPOT
2455 Paces Ferry Road
Atlanta, Georgia 30339
800-553-3199 (U.S.)
800-668-2266 (Canada)
www.homedepot.com
Tools, paint, wood, electrical, garden

HORTON BRASSES, INC.
49 Nooks Hill Road
Cromwell, Connecticut 06416
800-754-9127
www.horton-brasses.com
Hardware for antique furniture;
Hepplewhite, Chippendale and Victori-
an brass hardware; hand-forged iron
hardware

HOUSE OF TOOLS LTD.
100 Mayfield Common Northwest
Edmonton, Alberta, Canada T5P 4B3
800-661-3987
www.houseoftools.com
Woodworking tools and hardware

JESSEM TOOL COMPANY
124 Big Bay Point Road
Barrie, Ontario, Canada L4N 9B4
866-272-7492
www.jessem.com
Rout-R-Slide and Rout-R-Lift

KLINGSPOR'S WOODWORKING SHOP
P.O. Box 5069
Hickory, North Carolina 28603-5069
800-228-0000
www.woodworkingshop.com
Tools and supplies

KREG TOOL COMPANY
201 Campus Drive
Huxley, Iowa 50124
800-447-8638
www.kregtool.com
Pocket hole jigs and accessories

LANGEVIN & FOREST LTE.
9995 Boulevard Pie XI
Montreal, Quebec, Canada H1Z 3X1
800-889-2060
Tools, wood and books

LEE VALLEY TOOLS LTD.
P.O. Box 1780
Ogdensburg, New York 13669-6780
800-267-8735
www.leevalley.com
Fine woodworking tools and hardware

LIFT-TECH
25133 Avenue Tibbitts — B
Valencia, California 91355
661-702-9055
www.televisionlifts.com
Television lifts

LOWE'S HOME IMPROVEMENT WAREHOUSE
P.O. Box 1111
North Wilkesboro, North Carolina 28656
800-445-6937
www.lowes.com
Tools, paint, wood, electrical, garden

PACKARD WOODWORKS INC.
P.O. Box 718
Tryon, North Carolina 28782
800-683-8876
www.packardwoodworks.com
Woodturning supplies

PANOLAM INDUSTRIES INTERNATIONAL, INC.
20 Progress Drive
Shelton, Connecticut 06484
800-672-6652
www.panolam.com
Particleboard supplier

PAXTON WOODCRAFTERS' STORE
4837 Jackson Street
Denver, Colorado 80216
800-332-1331
www.paxton-woodsource.com
Domestic and foreign hardwoods; ve-
neers; books and woodworking tools

PORTER-CABLE
4825 Highway 45 North
P.O. Box 2468
Jackson, Tennessee 38302-2468
800-487-8665
www.porter-cable.com
Woodworking tools

RICHELIEU HARDWARE
7900, West Henri-Bourassa
Ville St-Laurent, Quebec, Canada
H4S 1V4
800-619-5446 (U.S.)
800-361-6000 (Canada)
www.richelieu.com
Hardware supplies

ROCKLER WOODWORKING AND HARDWARE
4365 Willow Drive
Medina, Minnesota 55340
800-279-4441
www.rockler.com
Woodworking tools and hardware

S&G SPECIALTY FASTENERS, INC.
2420 Camino Ramon, Suite 320
San Ramon, California 94583
800-743-6916
www.quickscrews.com
Fasteners and drive bits

SEVEN CORNERS HARDWARE, INC.
216 West 7th Street
Saint Paul, Minnesota 55102
651-224-4859
www.7cornershdwe.com
Discount mail order; mostly power tools

TENRYU AMERICA, INC.
7964 Kentucky Drive, Suite 12
Florence, Kentucky 41042
800-951-7297
www.tenryu.com
Saw blades

TOOL TREND LTD.
140 Snow Boulevard
Concord, Ontario, Canada L4K 4C1
416-663-8665
Woodworking tools and hardware

UNIBOARD CANADA INC.
3080, Le Carrefour Boulevard, Suite 400
Laval, Quebec, Canada H7T 2R5
800-263-5240
www.uniboard.com
Particleboard and MDF supplier

VAN DYKE'S RESTORERS
P.O. Box 278
39771 South Dakota Highway 34
Woonsocket, South Dakota 57385
800-558-1234
www.vandykes.com
Restoration hardware and supplies

VAUGHAN
11414 Maple Avenue
Hebron, Illinois 60034
815-648-2446
www.vaughanmfg.com
Hammers and other tools

WILKE MACHINERY COMPANY
3230 North Susquehanna Trail
York, Pennsylvania 17402-9716
800-235-2100
www.wilkemach.com
Woodworking tools

WOLFCRAFT NORTH AMERICA
333 Swift Road
Addison, Illinois 60101
630-773-4777
www.wolfcraft.com
Woodworking hardware and accessories

WOODCRAFT
P.O. Box 1686
Parkersburg, West Virginia 26102-1686
800-225-1153
www.woodcraft.com
Woodworking hardware and accessories

WOODWORKER'S HARDWARE
P.O. Box 180
Sauk Rapids, Minnesota 56379-0180
800-383-0130
www.wwhardware.com
Woodworking tools and accessories; finishing supplies; books and plans

WOODWORKER'S SUPPLY
1108 North Glenn Road
Casper, Wyoming 82601
800-645-9292
www.woodworker.com
Woodworking tools and accessories; finishing supplies; books and plans

WORKSHOP SUPPLY
P.O. Box 160
100 Commissioners Street, East
Embro, Ontario, Canada N0J 1J0
800-387-5716
www.workshopsupply.com
Woodworking tools; Jimmy Jigs

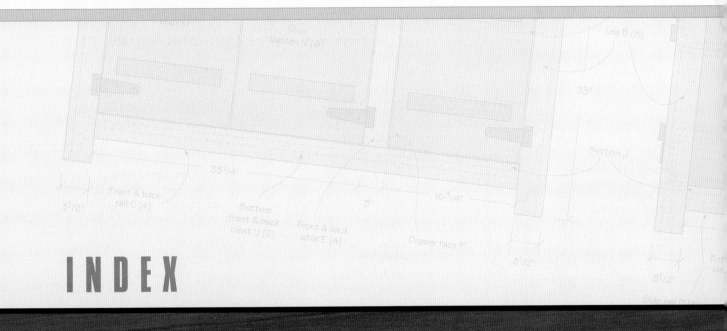

INDEX

The Best Woodworking Projects come from Popular Woodworking Books!

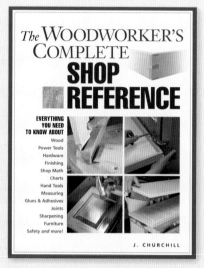

The ultimate one-stop shop reference for woodworkers of all skill levels and specialties! The Woodworker's Complete Shop Reference provides instant access to solutions for every woodworking dilemma. You'll find helpful information on a variety of key topics including wood, hardware, shop math, routers, hand tools, power tools, adhesives, joints, sharpening, furniture and much more!

ISBN 1-55870-632-1, paperback, 144 pages, #70579-K

Craft fine furniture featuring popular styles from the 18th century to today. No matter what your skill level, you'll learn how to build 10 elegant furniture projects start-to-finish. Easy-to-follow instructions, step-by-step photos, and guidelines for choosing woods and veneers make it easy to create cherished pieces.

ISBN 1-55870-645-3, paperback, 128 pages, #70593-K

Plan, design, construct and install your own complete handmade kitchen, from simple cabinets and over-sink cupboards to lazy-Susan shelving, stemware storage and more. These start-to-finish guidelines make it easy. You'll also find practical information on kitchen design, material selection and tool shortcuts.

ISBN 1-55870-676-3, paperback, 128 pages, #70626-K

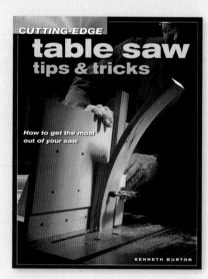

Ken Burton illustrates just how important and efficient your table saw can be with dozens of tricks, techniques and jigs that cover the entire range of what a table saw can do, everything from crafting precision joinery to accurately cutting pieces to size. Each technique is easy-to-do, safe to execute, and certain to save you time and money.

ISBN 1-55870-623-2, paperback, 128 pages, #70569-K

These books and other fine Popular Woodworking titles are available from your local bookstore, online supplier or by calling 1-800-448-0915.